A Dirty Sink, A Bug, and Squirrels: God Speaks

Mary Beth Powell

A Dirty Sink, A Bug, and Squirrels: God Speaks

True Stories of Finding God in Everyday Places

from
Warren and Mary Beth Powell

A Dirty Sink, A Bug, and Squirrels:
God Speaks
*True Stories of Finding God
in Everyday Places*

Copyright© 2006
Warren and Mary Beth Powell
Henderson, Texas

All rights reserved. No part of this publication may be reproduced in any form, stored in any retrieval system, or transmitted electronically or by any other means-----except for the inclusion of brief quotations in a review, without prior written permission from the authors or publishers.

Library of Congress Control Number: 2006907222
ISBN: 978-0-9788413-0-0

Printed in the U.S.A. by Morris Publishing
3212 East Highway 30
Kearney, NE 68847
1-800-650-7888

The use of references or quoted verses from various Bibles in this publication is not necessarily an endorsement of a specific version or translation in its entirety.

Scripture taken from the New King James Version®. Copyright © 1982 by Thomas Nelson, Inc. Used by permission. All rights reserved.

Scripture quotations taken from the New American Standard Bible®,Copyright © 1960, 1962, 1963, 1968, 1971, 1972, 1973,1975, 1977, 1995 by The Lockman Foundation Used by permission. (www.Lockman.org)

Scripture taken from the *Amplified Bible*, Copyright © 1954, 1958, 1962, 1964, 1965, 1987 by The Lockman Foundation. Used by permission.

Scripture taken from the HOLY BIBLE, NEW INTERNATIONAL VERSION®. NIV®. Copyright© 1973, 1978, 1984 by International Bible Society. Used by permission of Zondervan. All rights reserved.

Scripture quotations are taken from the Holy Bible, New Living Translation, copyright ©1996. Used by permission of Tyndale House Publishers, Inc., Wheaton, Illinois 60189. All rights reserved.

Scripture quotations marked (CEV) are from the Contemporary English Version Copyright © 1991, 1992, 1995 by American Bible Society, Used by Permission.

Scripture references marked TLB are taken from *The Living Bible*, copyright © 1971 by Tyndale House Publishers, Wheaton, Illinois 60187. All rights reserved.

The Message by Eugene H. Peterson, copyright (c) 1993, 1994, 1995, 1996, 2000, 2001, 2002. Used by permission of NavPress Publishing Group. All rights reserved.

Scripture references marked KJV are taken from the Holy Bible, King James Version.

For You, Lord

With this book, we lift You up and honor You, our Lord God Almighty, for turning into good every wrong road taken, every missed turn, and every wrong decision we have made.

We bless You for everything that has happened along the way to our being together and at this point in our lives, including all of the painful experiences You have helped us through.

May this book offer a thread of Your truth, love, comfort, and healing for those whose eyes search its pages for help.

We also pray that these stories will challenge others, just as they have challenged us, to listen more attentively to the different ways You speak to each of us today.

TABLE OF CONTENTS

Introduction	11
The Story of Sonbeams	13
Being a HIT and Mary Beth's Sink	15
Getting In and Out of God's Groove	18
Jesus and the Rusk County Library	21
The Squirrels Are Just a-Diggin'	22
She Called Me Mr. Mary Beth	24
Cream in My Coffee	26
He Doesn't Count the Minutes	28
Lord, Please Don't Hold the Chicken	30
Take One Pill, 2 Times a Day	32
That's Not Sin, You Know	34
Wait Till the Coffee Is Ready	36
Puppies, Fleas, and God	38
Holding My Hand over My Other Ear	40
Weighing in with God	42
Mary Beth and the Office Ants	44
Peek-a-Boo	46
Your Leaves Don't Have to be Dry	48
There I Was in a Zip Lock Bag	50
My Very Next Step	53
A Brush and Paint	56
Disconnected	58

Their Votes Don't Count	60
Fillin' Up the Water Bowls	62
Trapped!	64
Between the Biscuit and Me	67
Are You Being Friendly or Are You Married?	70
Come Here, Delilah	72
There Is No Life in the Fence	74
In a Dog's Body	77
It's Not Always Opportunity	80
A Tree on the Next Island	82
I Wanna Be a Cloud	84
Not a Night Light, Please	86
A Squirrel Is on Our Cable	88
The Water Is Always Hot	91
Bailey and Delilah	92
How's Your Reception?	94
Throwing Away Cold Coffee	96
What's Making You Dance Today?	99
The Grasp	101
About Warren and Mary Beth, the Authors	106
Warren's Story	108
What About This Jesus?	116
Alphabetical List of Titles	118
My Thoughts (for making notes)	120

Introduction

The stories in <u>A Dirty Sink, A Bug, and Squirrels: God Speaks</u> are our own true experiences. Our desire in this book is to share with you what we believe that God has shown us through the everyday things around us. Our stories are intended to encourage, challenge, and benefit others in this difficult world in which we live.

Jesus taught using things the common people were familiar with, such as seeds, animals, fig trees, crops, vineyards, and birds. His parables show us how to love Him, love others, overcome obstacles, and have a personal, one-to-one relationship with Him.

We believe that God still uses everyday life experiences and situations to teach us His unwavering truths. Our stories are intended as little rays of light, originally written as Sonbeams, attempting to bring into focus much larger truths through everyday things around us.

He uses some surprising things from our everyday lives to teach us His eternal unwavering truths.......like a dirty sink to show us about sin and forgiveness, a bug on a sidewalk to show us about walking His path, cream in a cup of coffee as an example of spreading the joy we have in Him, just to name a few.

These simple things that happened to us are things that many readers will understand. We are learning to find God in places we wouldn't normally look and listen for Him a little differently than we are used to listening..... because God still speaks.

The Story of Sonbeams

Included in this book are many of the true stories we have written of finding God in everyday places. We have emailed them to many readers over the past six years. Through Sonbeams, we wanted to share with others some of the simple things of God that we have learned through the ordinary things and events around us.

Following the death of my wife, Jean, in August of 1999, people told me how she had helped them in many ways. She was a beautiful person and a thoughtful lady. She was loved and appreciated, but she had no idea how much she touched other people's lives.

Jean did not realize what an impact her life made on others. If she had been able to listen at family visitation the night before her funeral, or even at her funeral, she would have heard the kind words of love and appreciation others said about her. She just never knew it, though.

I (Warren) started writing and emailing Sonbeams to a few friends and family, hoping to encourage and lift them up. For a while, Jean had a little Christian book distribution business named Sonbeams. Mary Beth and I use that name now to honor Jean's memory.

Sonbeams readers often forward our stories to friends and family. We have heard that some of our stories have been read at funerals and printed in church bulletins. Some of them have even been used as study material in a ladies group study in Cape Town, South Africa. To God be all the Glory!

Email addresses of our readers are never shared, seen, or sold.

To comment or subscribe free of charge, please email us:
warren@sonbeams.org

Being a HIT and Mary Beth's Sink

To begin with, you need a little history about me. I was widowed until March 2003, then the Lord joined Mary Beth and me together into one package....one wonderful marriage with Him. For the previous couple of years, my habits around the house were, to say the least, somewhere between helter-skelter and very organized.....depending upon things such as the wind, time of day, how sleepy I was, if it was raining, who was coming over.....all sorts of very valuable input.

When I became a HIT, my life began to change for the better. Oh yeah, perhaps it would help if I shared with you what I am talking about. A HIT stands for "Husband-in-Training." Please understand being a HIT is a very positive thing, but definitely not a one-semester course. It is a lifelong experience for the better and, when carefully studied, doing all the homework and reviews and taking notes and a lot of prayer.....being a HIT is always for the best.

Having said that, let's get down to what this piece is about: Mary Beth's sink. When we got married, we began living in Henderson, Texas, in Mary Beth's home. Her mother and father had lived in the house for over 20 years, leaving it to Mary Beth after her father's death. Although there is the 40-minute drive to Tyler Junior College daily for our teaching jobs, any inconvenience at all is minor compared to the many benefits of small-town life.

Mary Beth's sinks are very white. So white that when I moved here, I often wondered how she kept them so clean and new-looking. It didn't take long for me to find out how she does it.

A Dirty Sink, A Bug, and Squirrels: God Speaks

A couple of times I emptied my coffee cup into the sink, rinsed out the cup, then placed it in the left side of the sink to move it to the dishwasher later. Mary Beth was very gentle in helping me to learn to totally rinse out the sink also.....even to splashing water where any wayward drops of coffee might have tried to hang on to the wall of the sink for dear life.

She taught me that the longer any spots stay on the white porcelain, the harder it is to get the stain off. Also, the more often I forget, the more the forgetting becomes a habit. I get used to seeing the stains, then I get so used to seeing the stains that they become almost second-nature to being there. They would not bother me and after a while I wouldn't care about washing them off the sink. It's like it would become a circle of continual staining.....rather than simply taking care to cleanse the sink as often as I use it.

LaDonna Johnson once shared with me a technique she used when she had to clean her home in a hurry. She called it a Death Clean. Before I got married that is what I usually used on my own sink and home when someone was coming over. However, as a result of this wonderful Husband-In-Training program, Mary Beth's sink stays very clean.....without having to give it a Death Clean.

So a few days ago, as I was using the little sprayer in the sink to dislodge some wild coffee spots, the Lord showed me that the spots were like little sins in my life and the way in which I sometimes tend to ignore little things in my own life that dot the landscape of my everyday living. They were things that I should simply take to Him as they occur instead of waiting until they pile up and I have to 'go heavily to God,' all burdened up. It is the daily time I spend with Him that is the most important, not the now-and-then Death Clean time of running in a panic to Him with a whole lot of confessing to do.

His living water cleans the most determined spot of sin by the washing of the Word. His Word....My participation. My confession.....His forgiveness. My repentance.....His grace. What more is there? No steel wool needed. No SOS pads. No toxic liquids. Just His love....daily washing away my confessed sin.

Being a HIT is one of the many pleasures of my life. God is so good to me.

My Thoughts _____

_____

_____

_____

_____

Getting In and Out of God's Groove

I awoke around 3:45 this morning. Before my accident on Thanksgiving, I would be up by 5-5:30 most mornings, getting a cup of coffee or tea, going out on the deck and enjoying the coming of dawn. Most of my writings were done during these early mornings with God.

Today is different though. This morning finds me sitting in my wheelchair at 4:15am in the courtyard of HealthSouth Rehabilitation Hospital here in Tyler, listening to the night birds singing their goodnight melodies to one another. At the same time, the morning birds are chiming in with "It's our turn next to celebrate the rising of the sun."

The air is a little heavy with moisture, suspended as if waiting in line to spread its coat on the grass and leaves like a thin coat of paint on an artist's canvas. I can see the wet shining like so many diamonds glittering with sparkles from streetlights across the lawn.

About 15 minutes ago I watched a bug leave the safety and security of the manicured grass near me, starting his journey across the expanse of the sidewalk where I am parked. He scurried along, coming to the indention of the straight line where 2 pieces of concrete are joined together. The bug then went down inside.

Ever so often the bug would climb up the side, look around, as if he were checking out all around it, then disappear from my view, going on to the other side of the sidewalk. Of course, whenever he crawls out to look around, his life is in danger of being seen by birds, frogs or lizards, which could cost him his life. Too many times of peeping out and he would not ever reach his final destination.

As I watched, he reminded me of myself in some areas of my daily walk through life. I start out deciding to do something, just like the bug decided to cross the sidewalk. I find myself choosing between the flat areas of my own "sidewalk," deciding on my own which direction I have to go, making choices based upon my situation. Instead, I could choose to get into the pathway that my creator has laid out for me [such as the builder did with the joints of the sidewalk].

Even then, just like the little bug, I climb out of where I am safest [God's hands], looking around to see if I can do better, or faster, than the journey I am taking. God created a pathway for me, through the valleys, over the mountains, through good times and bad, in order for me to arrive at my final destination holding hands with Jesus.

Unfortunately, there are times when I make decisions to do something, and then ask God to bless my choices. That's the reverse order of God's way. I am to pray first, make my choices based on His Word, and then praise Him for what He has done and what He will do.

Just like the little bug, I get impatient or bored with progress or timing in certain areas and climb out of the groove, looking around for shortcuts or something that feels better than doing it God's way. Perhaps the saddest part is that mostly I don't even realize I am doing it! And it subjects me to so much danger and heartache. But I get in such a hurry.

A Dirty Sink, A Bug, and Squirrels: God Speaks

Lord Jesus, I know You have a plan for each and every one of us. Help us follow Your instructions rather than wander around the sidewalks of our lives, hoping maybe to make it across someday.

Thank You for making the way to You possible. We cannot do it on our own. Only in You are our lives secured.

My Thoughts _____

_____

_____

_____

Jesus and the Rusk County Library

Our life is a bit on the hectic side right now, so the two library books I had checked out did not get read by the due date. I put on my errand list to take them back on Tuesday, the day they were due, but – you know it – it didn't happen until Wednesday – and they were late.

The lady at the counter was very nice as she took my 20 cents (10 cents per day per book – I love my small-town life!) and let me check the books out for another 2 weeks. When she entered the payment of my fine into the computer, it cleared my record with the library as though I had never had an overdue book.

My slate is completely wiped clean – you know, the way our sins are completely wiped clean by the blood of Jesus – once and for all. When God forgives, there is no record remaining to condemn us for what Jesus' blood has already paid for.

So how 'bout it? Got any overdue library books, that is, unconfessed sin? The Great Librarian is ready to wipe your slate clean, just for the asking.

Into His Word

"On the other hand, if we admit our sins--make a clean breast of them--he won't let us down; he'll be true to himself. He'll forgive our sins and purge us of all wrongdoing."
                    1 John 1:9 The Message

The Squirrels are Just a-Diggin'

We're slowly going to and fro in our swing here in our front yard. It's Saturday and since we don't have to be at TJC teaching Math this morning, we're simply sharing some time with one another, watching the birds and squirrels in our yard getting ready for winter.

The squirrels are especially fun to watch as they busily bury acorns and nuts in one location or another. I've often wondered just how a squirrel chooses where to bury something.

He or she will go to one spot, dig a little, suddenly spring to a different spot and bury the acorn there instead. That's why we see squirrels just a-diggin' a lot of the time, burying or diggin' up their food all over the place.

Just like those squirrels, you and I need to bury something, too. It is far more valuable than food and we shouldn't bury it in the ground. Our treasure is the Word of God and it belongs in our hearts, not on our bookshelves.

We need His Word when things are going wrong. We cherish it when everything's going right. We rejoice in it from morning till night. God's Word lifts us up, brings us joy, offers us peace, and guides us in our everyday lives.

Just like the squirrels that dig and bury throughout the day, you and I should remember and meditate upon God's Word throughout the day, too. His Word sheds light upon every path we will ever walk and helps guide us down the rocky roads we encounter.

When you see a squirrel burying an acorn or digging up something, remember.......that is really a picture of you and me......and God's Word.... never failing.......buried in our hearts.

Into His Word

"Your word I have hidden in my heart, that I might not sin against You."   Psalm 119:11 New King James Version

"Everything's falling apart on me, GOD; put me together again with your Word."   Psalm 119:107 The Message

"Your word is a lamp to my feet and a light for my path."
     Psalm 119:105 New International Version

"Your teachings are wonderful, and I respect them all. Understanding your word brings light to the minds of ordinary people. I honestly want to know everything you teach."
     Psalm 119:129 Contemporary English Version

"All Scripture is inspired by God and is useful to teach us what is true and to make us realize what is wrong in our lives. It straightens us out and teaches us to do what is right. It is God's way of preparing us in every way, fully equipped for every good thing God wants us to do."
     2 Timothy 3:16-17 New Living Translation

She Called Me Mr. Mary Beth

I was visiting one of Mary Beth's math classes and asked her students if they knew my name. A lady on the front row spoke up and she called me Mr. Mary Beth. We all had a really good laugh. They know Mary Beth and I are bonded, married; and that was good enough for me.

I am known as Dad, Mr. P, Warren, PapaBear, Sir Snack, Father, Teach, Mr. Powell, Warren A (my Mom calls me this), English Prof, and most recently one of our daughters has started calling me W, like the President of the United States.

Each name I am called is special, but for a different reason. However, the one that is above all others, stored highest in the treasure room of my heart, is the one God calls me: His.

His eyes are upon me everywhere. No matter who I am with, or how I am living a part of my life (husband, teacher, father, writer, friend, or other things). The dearest thing to me is to know that God calls me: His.

In the light: His
In the shadows: His
In the darkness: His
In my classroom: His
At church: His
At the park: His
Driving in heavy traffic: His
Spending time with our children: His
Playing with our grandchildren: His
During my 48-day coma: His
Celebrating in joyous praise and worship: His

Walking anywhere hand-in-hand with Mary Beth: His
The Lord of All calls me: His!

And when I leave this earthly body of aches and scars galore to stand before Him……my hope for all eternity is to hear Jesus' voice say, "Mine." He loves me. It is up to me to love Him in return and to daily praise Him for loving me.

Being His is for each one of us. That assurance only comes from having a personal relationship with Jesus Christ that is, being born again. Every person who is born again He calls child, He calls friend, but the very best is still: His.

Just think of it……..is there anything you'd rather hear than the Lord of Heaven and Earth calling you: His.

Into His Word

"You know when I am resting or when I am working, and from heaven you discover my thoughts. You notice everything I do and everywhere I go. I can't understand all of this! Such wonderful knowledge is far above me. Where could I go to escape from your Spirit or from your sight?

"If I were to climb up to the highest heavens, you would be there. If I were to dig down to the world of the dead you would also be there. Or suppose I said, 'I'll hide in the dark until night comes to cover me over.' But you see in the dark because daylight and dark are all the same to you.

"Nothing about me is hidden from you! I was secretly woven together deep in the earth below, Look deep into my heart, God, and find out everything I am thinking. Don't let me follow evil ways, but lead me in the way that time has proven true."
        Verses, Psalm 139, Contemporary English Version

Cream in My Coffee

Have you heard the song which goes something like "I've got the joy, joy, joy, joy down in my heart, down in my heart, down in my heart; I've got the joy, joy, joy, joy down in my heart, down in my heart to stay"? It's a pretty old one, but maybe you are familiar with it.

As I was getting ready to go out on my deck this morning, I got myself a cup of coffee to take with me. As I poured a little cream into the cup, the cream didn't blend into the rest of the coffee. The coffee and the cream stayed separate. I had a spoon in my hand, but held off stirring it.

I started to stir my coffee, but I waited. What I saw reminded me very much of the song. Those words about having the "joy down in my heart" hit home with me.

I do have that joy down in my heart. It is the joy of the Lord and from the Lord. There is none like it anywhere. It is a great gift from him and a great blessing. Many people I know have that same joy from the Lord in their hearts. Maybe you do, too.

Let's get back to the coffee and cream, though. Remember how the coffee had to be stirred up before it blended everything together? And even though I poured the cream into the coffee, it stayed mainly in one spot?

Well, I think that is what happens to the joy in our lives. Just because we have the joy of the Lord, until it is stirred up within us, until it literally overflows into the rest of our life, it just sits there. Sure it helps us, especially around our own friends. However, anyone can be joyful around people they know.

When we keep joy 'under wraps' so to speak, I think we are misusing one of the gifts God has given us. He gives us joy to use and spread around. What about all the others with whom we come in contact......in grocery lines, in movie theaters, on our jobs or those we simply pass in malls or stores? They need that same joy we experience, too.

There is a song that is sung mostly around Christmas that expresses what I am trying to say. It goes "Joy to the world, the Lord has come". Therein lies our joy. He has come.

What better news...what better joy? Let us live our lives so that all others see that same joy......then they may even ask us about where we get our joy. Wouldn't that make a wonderful story we could share with them?

Into His Word

"May the God of hope fill you with all joy and peace as you trust in Him, so that you may overflow with hope by the power of the Holy Spirit."
       Romans 15:13 New International Version

"No one lights a lamp and puts it in a place where it will be hidden, or under a bowl. Instead he puts it on its stand, so that those who come in may see the light."
       Luke 11:33 New International Version

He Doesn't Count the Minutes

A short while ago the sun drifted westward and slowly buried itself in the midst of the grove of trees at the end of our block. The chill of this night air is one of God's ways to remind me that the times of writing while sitting out front in just shorts and a T-shirt are drawing to a close.

Right now the mosquitoes are around our swing, using my arms and legs for their Campground and PlayArea. Overhead the moon is very visible, yet it appears split down the middle like a pie, half in darkness and half in light. It's like God is sharing some humor with me.

Today in Math class we began fractions. I used a circle with a line down it, just like the moon is tonight. And now God and I are sharing the same thing. I just love my times with Him.

Some people mistakenly think that time with God has to produce a great spiritual change, or involve praying for something, or learning a lesson. Yet many times, quality time with the Father is spent just sensing His majesty and giving Him the glory only He deserves.

Other times it's simply a handful of minutes of our life, once again letting God be God while we sit back in awe of who He is. We do not have to be in prayer, or confession, or repentance, or even saying a single word. Time with God is anytime we are recognizing Him as the one true God, the giver of Life.

Whether our time with Him is thirty minutes or simply a mere vision of God's presence in someone or something around us, we need to know that He doesn't count the minutes. His desire is for each of us to spend time worshipping Him in spirit and in truth......praising Him as the great I AM.

We will never know what God has in store for us unless we show up to share time with Him. In His Holy presence, an hour can be like one moment.......and one moment can be like eternity.

<u>Into His Word</u>

"If I flew on morning's wings to the far western horizon, You'd find me in a minute--you're already there waiting!"
                              Psalm 139:9 The Message

My Thoughts _____

_____

_____

_____

_____

Lord, Please Don't Hold the Chicken

It happened a couple of weeks ago in the little artsy-craftsy East Texas town of Edom. We were eating with Shannon at The Shed, a center of great food, wonderful wait staff, and customers who visit with one another as good friends. In fact, that Friday night, the chalkboard menu on the wall showed 8 different kinds of pie, and since Joy has nicknamed me Sir Snack, you can imagine I felt right at home.

Then we heard it. A lady at the next table told her waitress that she wanted "a Grilled Chicken Sandwich, but hold the chicken." The waitress asked to be sure she understood what the woman wanted, and sure enough, all she wanted was the bread, the mayo, the Swiss cheese, the onions......all grilled.....but she really did not want the grilled chicken. She only wanted the trimmings, and that was what she got.

On the way home, we laughed a lot about the lady's sandwich request. Then, as we talked, our conversation widened to other things in our lives that we treat somewhat in the same way. One example is how we choose our friends, our dates, our spouses, or even our god.

When I was growing up, the things people most highly esteemed in each other were respect, integrity, a person's word, and faithfulness; they really meant something. Where did these things go, you might ask? They haven't gone anywhere. They are from God and have been with us from the beginning of time......and are here for you and for me.

Unfortunately, through advertising, TV and radio, magazines, and the internet, many people today are drawn to only the trimmings of life.......those of temporary and fleeting value. These include such things as who has the best body, the fanciest car, the most money, or is thought to be a great athlete or popular singer.

Looking around us, it appears most people are very willing to accept just the trimmings. The lady who wanted a Grilled Chicken Sandwich did not want the most highly valued part, the chicken, so she settled for only the less important, and in doing so, she missed out on the best.

Talking about this brought to my mind a couple of questions: In any of my relationships, am I settling for just the trimmings? Have I slowly slid off the menu of life and now put more importance in the add-ons instead of the real, permanent, deep-down values in a person that really count?

Heavenly Father, help me see through the veil of shine and glitter that this world waves before me. Let me see and value those things that You hold in high regard. I no longer need or want to desire just the trimmings of life. Lord, please don't hold the chicken.

Into His Word

"Turn my eyes away from worthless things; preserve my life according to your word."
                    Psalms 119:37 New International Version

Take 1 Pill, 2 Times a Day

One of Mary Beth's students gave her a basket of goodies this week for her birthday. In it were bottles of Ozarka water and a bottle of Ginkgo Biloba pills. This morning we decided to start taking the pills.

The instructions read, "Take 1 tablet, 2 times a day". We got a bottle of Ozarka, Mary Beth's favorite; I took a pill, put it in my mouth, and took a drink of water. I then took the pill out of my mouth, and told her, "Okay, I took the pill once, now I'll take it the 2nd time." I was just making a joke, so we laughed. I love the way she laughs at my jokes.

A few minutes later I realized that there was a lot more to the pill incident than just a good laugh. It had a purpose and a reason this morning for us and we were to share it with you.

The Bible teaches us what God desires of us and how we are to live for Him. We are to praise God in all things and never to put anyone or anything above Him. Next comes our own family.....not our job, not our friends, not our own needs or desires. Sometimes we get these things out of order, though.

Far too often we say things to ourselves and to others that are just like that first pill I pretended to take. I didn't swallow the pill; all I did was to fool Mary Beth into believing me. What I did had no effect deep down inside.......it was wasted because I didn't swallow it. It didn't become a part of me.

"I'm trying the best I can do." "I'm doing this all for you." "You are the most important person in the world to me." How often do these words, or others like them, come from our lips, but just like the pill I didn't swallow, the words were just to fool someone else, to keep them happy or off our backs. In some cases, we say things only to keep others from knowing how we really feel.

What we write or what we say, even those things we just hint about, all of them are words that we swallow and words that are real and meaningful to those to whom we are talking. Like it or not, we are always representing God to others.

The God we serve is Love; He is the God of truth and of honesty. He knows that our words and thoughts are proven through our actions. He is never fooled by the 'fake swallowing the pill' trick. He knows.

We are to test every word that comes out of our mouths. And when those times come that we are tempted to say things without meaning them, we need to ask the Lord for help. He is the source of living water that makes it possible for us to speak truth and love to those around us and for us to follow through with actions that validate our words.

His fountain of life is never-ending and is available for all who thirst for it. He will never disappoint anyone. Just step up and take a sip of His water........and be sure to swallow.

<u>Into His Word</u>

"A tree is identified by the kind of fruit it produces. Figs never grow on thorn bushes or grapes on bramble bushes. A good person produces good deeds from a good heart, and an evil person produces evil deeds from an evil heart. Whatever is in your heart determines what you say."
                      Luke 6:44-46 New Living Translation

That's Not Sin, You Know

That's not sin, you know. At least that's what I think the Holy Spirit whispered to me this morning. I opened the garbage bin to see if the garbage needed to be emptied (another of the things I get joy out of doing for Mary Beth).

I hesitated momentarily; after all, it was only 2/3 full, and while I was looking at it, well, that was when I heard a voice within me saying, "That's not sin, you know, Warren." When I heard that, I stopped and listened.

"Many people think that sin is like garbage; that they have to wait until they have a lot of sin before they confess their wrongs. Or else, they wait until it really stinks. Sin is not like garbage. Sin needs to be dealt with continually, because I cannot stand any of it."

I hurriedly emptied our garbage and knew I had to go out to our front yard swing and share this with you. As I began to write, I learned there was more.

"You see, what someone considers just a little bit of sin, well, to Me.....that's a lot. And whether it smells or not isn't important. It all brings a stench to My nostrils. Many people believe that unless their sin is at a certain level, it doesn't need to be dealt with (like the garbage). But any sin is too much.

"I am here to help you. Whenever anyone asks me, I will always expose their sin to them. Here is why I do it: Sin blocks and hinders My relationship with each of My children.....and that is one of the reasons I hate sin. I do not want anything to come between us. Sin gets in the way;

therefore it has to be emptied out constantly. So see, garbage is not like sin."

And now, for the rest of the story *(apologies to Paul Harvey):* While Warren was out front writing about garbage and sin, unknown to him, the following was happening in the kitchen to me (Mary Beth).

I was fixing our lunch---the plan was a couple of sandwiches. I had seen a package of lunchmeat in the refrigerator left over from the weekend; I had made a mental note to use it soon. Rummaging through the meat/cheese drawer revealed a science experiment growing in our Swiss cheese---over the trash to throw it away!

Oh my, there's a new trash bag…..that means Warren just emptied the trash and I'm going to put this spoiled stuff in here----it will get stinky soon. I really should walk this out to the outside trash can, but I don't really want to go to all the trouble to take just this little bit out…..

You see, when garbage smells, everyone knows it is there. However, sin can be quietly subtle or internally rampant in a person's life, all the while unseen to anyone else but God. He loves each of us…….and He can always tell the difference between our garbage and our sin.

Into His Word

"If we say that we have not sinned, we are fooling ourselves, and the truth isn't in our hearts. But if we confess our sins to God, he can always be trusted to forgive us and take our sins away. If we say that we have not sinned, we make God a liar, and his message isn't in our hearts."
1 John 1:8-10 Contemporary English Bible

Wait Till the Coffee Is Ready

Whipped cream. It'll do me in every time. I wasn't even thinking about something to drink tonight at Life Group until Christine walked into the room with that whipped cream floating around at the top of her coffee. She sorta waved it in my direction and I just couldn't resist getting me some.

In the kitchen, some of the others were just pouring out the last of the coffee. As usual we were at Henri and Shirley's home, so Henri volunteered to make another pot. He carefully measured the coffee and water, and then went see if the Astros had won their playoff game.

I stood there patiently waiting for the coffee to brew. I noticed that he had forgotten to turn on the coffeemaker. Christine pushed its button and it began to brew (finally!). I waited as long as I could, that is, until the pot was about 1/3 full. I had to act fast. As I pulled the pot away from underneath the coffeemaker, the coffee kept on dripping, and one drop after another sizzled aloud as it hit the hotplate below. I laughed at my impatience; after all, it was just coffee for goodness sake.

I then took my coffee into the living room where we were gathering for togetherness in praise and worship. As Andy began to play his guitar and lead us in song, the Lord gave me an inner nudge, telling me that what just happened in the kitchen had more to do with Him than with my cup of coffee.

He said that my coffeepot experience was a carbon copy of how many of us respond to Him. You see, He always has a plan in process, yet in our haste to hurry things up, we take into our hands what we believe is His answer before He is finished and when we do, we make a mess of it, just like I did with the coffeepot.

We have gotten so accustomed to instant everything, that most of the time we expect God to do everything instantly, too, including answering our prayers. He has great plans for us and He is showing us the way, but we don't wait upon Him. We decide to jump in and take things into our own hands, thinking He is through with our situation.....yet He is not. I can just picture Him telling me over and over again, "Not yet, Warren. I'm not finished with that."

I didn't wait till the coffee was ready, so it didn't taste the way Henri wanted it to---and that wasn't such a big deal. However, anytime we take the bull by the horns, ahead of God when He is not through dealing with a situation in our life.....well, that IS a big deal.

We want all of what God has for us, not just part of it. None of us wants to intentionally cut Him off from operating in our life. He is always working things to our best interest. We must remember to wait patiently on Him. He is always only a whisper or a thought away......with His answer.

<u>Into His Word</u>

"With all your heart you must trust the LORD and not your own judgment. Always let him lead you, and he will clear the road for you to follow."
                Proverbs 3:5-6 Contemporary English Version

"We know that God is always at work for the good of everyone who loves him."
                Romans 8:28 Contemporary English Version

Puppies, Fleas, and God

Ten puppies. That's how many Mary Beth and I bathed yesterday, getting them ready to sell. They were a Great Dane and Dalmatian mix. Mostly black, some had splotches of white while others were white with black spots on their feet.

Ever tried to find fleas on a black puppy? You must either examine the puppy very closely or catch the puppy scratching. After we washed each one, we checked the water for fleas. We love our puppies and don't want them to suffer.

The only way to know if a puppy has been cleansed effectively and is free of fleas is by the way the puppy behaves. Does the puppy still scratch? Has the puppy's behavior changed?

The way that God changes our lives resembles trying to check for fleas on a puppy. We cannot always recognize sin by simply looking, in fact, most sin is hidden like fleas on our black puppies.

Other people cannot tell if anything is wrong in our life by looking at the way we are dressed, or what we do for a living, or how much money we have. Others don't know the depth of our struggles just by asking us, either. Sometimes we will lie to our friends if we are too embarrassed, discouraged, or depressed about what we are doing.

However, all the while God sees everything in our life, as nothing is hidden from Him. God loves us and does not want us to suffer from sin in our lives. He knows the only thing that will really cleanse us of our sin is the blood of His Son, Jesus.

When we repent and receive God's cleansing, our behavior changes for the best……every time. Just like getting rid of those fleas.

Into His Word

"Because of the sacrifice of the Messiah, his blood poured out on the altar of the Cross, we're a free people--free of penalties and punishments chalked up by all our misdeeds. And not just barely free, either. Abundantly free!"
Ephesians 1:7 The Message

"Blessed are they whose transgressions are forgiven, whose sins are covered. Blessed is the man whose sin the Lord will never count against him."
Romans 4:7-8 New International Version

"He's set us up in the kingdom of the Son he loves so much, the Son who got us out of the pit we were in, got rid of the sins we were doomed to keep repeating."
Colossians 1:13, 14 The Message

My Thoughts _____

_____

_____

_____

_____

Holding My Hand over My Other Ear

Morning just isn't the same up here on the 20th floor balcony of our hotel in San Antonio. We see a lot more than from our porch back in Henderson. The early sounds of a city begin coming to life, floating upwards from down around the Riverwalk.

As I sit with my eyes closed, the sounds seem to separate themselves and I play a game with myself, trying to figure out what sound goes with what is happening. Here I am, 20 stories in the air.....surely I couldn't hear that familiar beep, beep, beep. But it is what I had guessed......a trash truck backing down the street a little. It surprises me that amid all the sounds, that one tiny horn could still be heard.

Why couldn't God have installed a horn like that inside of me to warn me when I get off track from His path or when I find myself backing up....repeating some past sin again even though I know better. My life would be so much easier if He had a sort of beeper inside of me warning, 'no, stop, watch where you're going!'

If I could actually hear His voice in my ear, like the sound of that truck horn, well, I could try holding my hand over my other ear so that what He said wouldn't leak out of my head. However, God doesn't work that way. He speaks to my heart, just like He does to yours, in love.

And if God is 20 floors away when He speaks to me.......well, I will hear Him......that is, if I am listening.

Into His Word

"Good friend, take to heart what I'm telling you; collect my counsels and guard them with your life. Tune your ears to the world of Wisdom; set your heart on a life of Understanding......and here's why: GOD gives out Wisdom free, is plainspoken in Knowledge and Understanding."
Proverbs 2:1, 6 The Message

"Dear friend, listen well to my words; tune your ears to my voice. Keep my message in plain view at all times. Concentrate! Learn it by heart! Those who discover these words live, really live; body and soul, they're bursting with health."
Proverbs 4:20-22 The Message

My Thoughts _____

_____

_____

_____

_____

Weighing in with God

I have been weighing myself almost every morning in hopes that somehow there has been some change for the better in my weight just because I show up and step on the scales. Of course nothing is going to happen unless I do something to change the way I live.

Right now it's losing a pound here, gaining a pound there; consistently inconsistent. Whatever happens.......just happens. My weight won't change unless I change.

I cannot just say that I want to lose weight. If I really mean what I say, I will do something about how I eat and live. Whatever I do must include a commitment in every part of my daily life. When I am not losing weight, no one else is to blame; it is my own responsibility.

As I stepped on the scales yesterday, it occurred to me that many of us have another habit......one of weighing in with God........mostly on Sunday mornings. We hope to see some move of God just because we showed up. We look for a new enthusiasm towards God, a renewed joy, a better understanding of His word, or a deeper relationship with Jesus. When none is found, unfortunately we return to just doing the same things we have been doing.......yet still expecting change.

Just like when I want to lose weight, we must do more than simply show up at church, sing a song or two, sit in a pew, and listen to a sermon. It takes a commitment, a personal offering to God, both spiritually and physically, of every area in our life.

God's love actively moves over the face of all His creation. His fountain is always flowing for those of us who are seeking more of Him. If we are not getting more of God, no one else is to blame; it is our own responsibility.

God knows when we really mean business. We cannot hold anything back from Him. To try to hide something in our life from God would be like trying to weigh ourselves while holding on to a countertop for leverage; it will fool the scales, but we know it's a lie. God does not play such games.

My bathroom scales tell me only about my bodyweight in that second I am on them. Weighing in with God on a daily basis tells me about myself both now and for all eternity. I want less pounds. I want more God. Both are up to me.

Into His Word

"For the eyes of the LORD range throughout the earth to strengthen those whose hearts are fully committed to him."
    2 Chronicles 16:9 New International Version

"Obey God's message! Don't fool yourselves by just listening to it. If you hear the message and don't obey it, you are like people who stare at themselves in a mirror and forget what they look like as soon as they leave."
    James 1:22-24 Contemporary English Version

My Thoughts _____

_____

Mary Beth and the Office Ants

Mary Beth has been bothered with ants in her office on campus. Not fire ants, just the little pesky ones that parade up and down, around and around like they are showing off, somehow finding every tiny morsel anyone dropped.

Yesterday she decided to go into battle fully armed for this enemy. She purchased a number of those ant bait houses and put them around her office before we left for home.

This morning, as I was finishing breakfast and Mary Beth was fixing our lunches, she explained to me how the little ant bait houses work. You see, I thought the houses were simply traps that killed the ants when they went inside to get the bait, but I was wrong.

The bait attracts the ant and when the ant goes inside to get the bait, a slow-acting poison gets on the ant. Then, when that ant returns to its nest or whatever ants call home, the poison kills the other ants, too. That way the poison spreads and kills more than just one ant at-a-time.

In fact, we fall for the same thing. We go after some bait this world offers us, but we get a lot more than we bargained for. Just like with those ants, the poisons that are with the bait attach themselves to us.

Whatever we come in contact with…….stays in us and with us in one way or another; if not physically, then emotionally; if not emotionally, then in our mind; if not in our mind, then in our heart. After all, the Word of God tells us that our battles are not physical, they are spiritual.

What we watch, what we say, how we do our job, what we listen to, what we do......when there is any poison in it......that poison becomes a part of us. We carry it with us everywhere, infecting everyone with whom we come in contact. That is what poison is supposed to do and does.......for ants.....and for you and me.

But how can we avoid the constant temptations and lies disguised as truths that the world offers us? What can we do? We are to turn our hearts and eyes to the living God who created us. He will never lead us to destruction.

Otherwise, we're just like those ants who grabbed the bait, but also carried that poison home with them. That's us, too, whether we want to admit it or not. The blood of Jesus Christ is our only hope to be cleansed of those poisons that God calls sin. Without Jesus alive and active in our lives, we will indeed die.....just like those ants in Mary Beth's office did.

Into His Word

"Don't become so well-adjusted to your culture that you fit into it without even thinking. Instead, fix your attention on God. You'll be changed from the inside out. Readily recognize what he wants from you, and quickly respond to it.

"Unlike the culture around you, always dragging you down to its level of immaturity, God brings the best out of you, develops well-formed maturity in you."

          Romans 12:2 The Message

Peek-a-Boo

It's a simply gorgeous afternoon in February. The sun is shining, the temperature is around 73º, some small breezes are playing chase in the air, and Mary Beth and I are just sitting in our front yard swing, eating BBQ sandwiches from Bob's. Wow, what a sweet time.

About five or six feet away, something on the ground catches my eye, but when I turn to look that direction, I can't find it. I pause for a minute, hoping to see what had attracted my attention; nothing seems to be there but grass. It is some kind of light, but what?

As I wait, one of the baby breezes bounces off the ground and suddenly the sunlight is reflected off of a single small piece of cellophane caught in the grass. The swirling, dancing air is using it for a partner, leaning it first one way, then another, like two dancers doing a tango.

The breeze flips that cellophane back and forth in such a way that sometimes it reflects the sun and sometimes it doesn't. When the material is not acting as a reflector, it simply blends in along with everything else around it. It has no life of its own; therefore it has no power to choose anything and is dependent upon what's going on around it to move it.

Too often we choose to simply react to circumstances just like that piece of cellophane, too, instead of responding to our God who lives within us. Our lives are to be a living testimony, showing Jesus Christ, the Son of God, to the rest of the world. Instead, many times, by our own choices, we simply become peek-a-boo believers. Now others see God reflected in our lives.....now they don't.

When this happens, when we give circumstances control over who we are or how we act, we are just like that piece of cellophane and simply blend into the world around us. When those around us cannot see Him in our lives, they will not be able to tell the difference between a child of God and a child of this world.

There is no middle ground. Either we are reflecting our Lord Jesus Christ, or we are simply blending in, being just like those who don't know Jesus Christ as their Savior.

God created us in His image to love Him and exhibit His love for others to see. His grace is displayed through our changed lives, demonstrating to those around us that hope in God is their one and only refuge in a lost and struggling world.

Being a peek-a-boo believer is our own individual decision every moment of every day. God has given us everything we need to succeed in Him. Through our dependence upon Him, each one of us can be an illustration of God's love in action and that His love is available to anyone who believes in Him.

Into His Word

"Once more Jesus addressed the crowd. He said, I am the Light of the world. He who follows Me will not be walking in the dark, but will have the Light which is Life."
John 8:12 New International Version

Make your light shine, so that others will see the good that you do and will praise your Father in heaven."
Matthew 5:14-16 Contemporary English Version

Your Leaves Don't Have to be Dry

What a great winter day! Temperature hovering around 45-50 degrees, hardly any wind and a cloudless sky. I really appreciate a good fire of burning leaves……..the smell, the warmth and most of all, to be able to watch the fire burn the leaves until nothing is left but ashes.

Last Saturday Crash, some friends, and I were around such a fire. We had a small pile left over from last week, so we added some more stuff before we lit the fire again. Many of the leaves were quite dry and ignited immediately. Others were wet and took quite a while to start burning.

Let's pretend for a minute that the leaves represent the sins in our life. Wouldn't it be a lot easier to simply rake all of our sins into a pile, pick them up and toss them to God so He could burn them up and they would disappear? We kinda do that anyway by giving them to Him to forgive when we confess and repent of them.

But there are sins that we stash away, hidden from view, wet with the water of deceptive denial. You see, the mistake we make is that we don't bring them to the fire because we think we can handle them. Maybe we are so ashamed of them that we think God will not be able to burn them with the rest. We mistakenly believe that God sorts through our sins, taking longer to forgive some than others.

Your leaves don't have to be dry. The leaves of sin in your life are as ready now as they will ever be. When it comes to sin, the fire of God's forgiveness instantly burns and disintegrates

A Dirty Sink, A Bug, and Squirrels: God Speaks

all the leaves, both dry and wet....then destroys all their ashes. Rake yours today; God wants to burn them all.

Into His Word

"If we claim to be without sin, we deceive ourselves and the truth is not in us. If we confess our sins, He is faithful and just and will forgive us our sins and purify us from all unrighteousness. If we claim we have not sinned, we make Him out to be a liar and His word has no place in our lives."
      1 John 1:8-10 New International Version

"The LORD is compassionate and gracious, slow to anger, abounding in love. He will not always accuse, nor will He harbor His anger forever; He does not treat us as our sins deserve or repay us according to our iniquities. For as high as the heavens are above the earth, so great is His love for those who fear him; as far as the east is from the west, so far has He removed our transgressions from us."
      Psalm 103:8-12 New International Version

My Thoughts _____

_____

_____

_____

_____

There I Was in a Zip Lock Bag

<u>Personal note from Mary Beth:</u> Warren wrote this piece in December 2002, when we were very first dating. It was probably the turning point of "how he won my heart" – a man who actually hears from and responds to God! What woman could resist that?

Since I do not use a lot of meat at one time, I have a habit of freezing it in zip lock storage bags. Sometimes I get in a hurry to freeze it and I forget to squeeze all the air from the bag. This was never more evident to me than yesterday morning.

I was trying to do lots of things at once [gee whiz, what a surprise], grabbed one of the bags that had a couple of frozen ham slices in it, and rather than mess up the microwave, I put a bowl in the sink. I placed the bag in the bowl and turned the hot water directly on the bag, wanting to defrost the ham quickly.

About four minutes later I came back to get my slices of ham. Unfortunately what I found was that I had grabbed one of the bags with a lot of air in it, and the bag with the still-frozen slices was simply floating around on the top of the water, with the very hot water pouring its full strength and heat onto the air-filled bag.

Although the water was very hot, the bowl was holding the water, and the bag was directly in line with the hot water, in other words where it was supposed to be, the ham remained very cold and frozen in most places. The Lord then said to me, "Warren, sometimes that ham inside that bag represents you, listening for My voice."

I sort of laughed to myself a little. Wondering where this

lesson was heading, I stopped scurrying around and took a quick quiet time....to listen. No matter what I was doing, it was not more important than hearing from Him...even if it was going to hurt.

The Lord continued, "Because sometimes you get puffed up a little, full of yourself maybe, pride or whatever, when I want to reach you, I can't. You can be in the right place, doing the right thing, listening to the right message or reading the right Bible verses, and because of the way you are thinking about things, because of things in your own life, what I want you to hear....it very simply will not touch you where I want to come into a closeness or intimacy with you."

I knew exactly what He meant. As that bag of ham with all that air floated aimlessly around on top of the water, with more hot water pouring directly down upon it...yes, I knew. Right place, right time, all right conditions....yet, because I had not 'emptied out myself', I could not receive what God had for me.

Lord, please open me up to Your touch and Your voice. Remind me of Your many verses that teach me that I must constantly empty myself of me and let You fill me with more and more of You. It is You, O Lord, with whom I seek intimacy....the closeness, the touch and indwelling that comes only from Your Holy Spirit....to bring me to truly abundant life in You. I am in a moment-by-moment learning process with You as my teacher.

Let me be as the virgins who came to get their pots filled...they brought them empty. Please let me never forget that You cannot fill anything that already has something else in it.

Daily inspire me to make and take that time to be with You....to repent of my sins and be refreshed as only You can do. I know I must empty myself of myself. Let me always remember that frozen ham in the zip lock bag as a reminder that You are always with me, trying to draw me into contact with You, especially with the frozen parts of my life.....deep down inside. Amen.

Into His Word

"A man's pride brings him low, but a man of lowly spirit gains honor."
Proverbs 29:23 New International Version

"Practically everything that goes on in the world—wanting your own way, wanting everything for yourself, wanting to appear important—has nothing to do with the Father. It just isolates you from him.
"The world and all its wanting, wanting, wanting is on the way out—but whoever does what God wants is set for eternity."
1 John 2:16 The Message

My Very Next Step

The wind was blowing the rain almost like little arrows shot from some archer hidden behind the trees over near Jenkins Hall. There I was underneath the second story extended roof of the Tyler Junior College Library, waiting for a short break in the storm. My destination was Potter Hall, the next building, only about 150 feet away.

It had been raining for a couple of hours, so the sidewalk had water covering it in most places. I had to make a dash for it, because many of my Math students were probably waiting for me. Umbrella in one hand, books and briefcase in the other, I became Gene Kelly...trying to dance my way across the campus to Potter's dry haven. Dancing is not what I did.

The wind pretended that my umbrella was not there. Raindrops joined forces to find the bottom of my slacks, then my shirt, finally my arms and face. I leaned the umbrella over further and further, until I could see only a few feet in front of me. The clouds, close friends of the wind and rain, were darkening the sky, so it was not an easy path for me to follow. I found myself almost bumping into people heading towards the library and other places.

Of course, I wanted to simply jump from the library porch to the porch at Potter Hall in one single burst of athletic wonderfulness, but that was impossible. I had to take it one step at a time....just like Jesus wants us to totally trust Him.

That wet, dreary morning, what that umbrella became to me is what the Lord wants to be for each one of us...to be our covering, our protection. You see, my path took me directly through the storm. There was no other way. Even with my umbrella for protection, the storm would not disappear. The same goes for the storms of our lives....they don't go away just because we have God with us.

When Peter walked on the water to Jesus, and Jesus had to help Peter stop from sinking, they walked back to the boat through the storm. After their safe arrival in the boat, only then did our Lord command the storm to cease...and of course, it did.

Yes, I got wet from the storm, even with a good umbrella that did not leak. But you know what? In time, everything that got wet dried out. When we go through our own life's storms, everything that was meant to hurt us or harm us or cause us grief....Jesus uses for our own good...even when we seemingly step in the mud, or wander off the sidewalk, or fall in water too deep for the tops of our shoes.

The Lord is our covering. However, He is way more than just that. And not just in times of storms. He wants us safely sheltered under His mighty wings. He wants us wrapped in the truth of His Word. He desires us to trust and holding high the mighty banner of His love and of His righteousness for all to see.

Please remember; I simply wanted to get to Potter Hall without getting soaked that morning. Instead, I was shown a very clear picture of God's plan for each one of us.....trusting in Him for each step we take in life.

You know what? I could have tried to run through the rain on my own...without an umbrella, or jacket, or some kind of protection over my books [my valuables at that time]. But that would be like not protecting my family from life's wind and rains that try to rip and tear us apart. On our own.....we can do nothing...nothing that really, really matters to those we love and who love us.

If I did try to make it without Him....the result would have been disastrous...just as it has been before. When I take it on myself to make the right decisions...or to go down my own path....without the Lord inside of me, it cannot work. Not for me. Not for you. Not for anyone.

I held on to that umbrella tightly that morning, but I must hold on to Jesus even more. Storms or great weather. Umbrella needed...or not. He knows the way I am to walk. All I have to do is trust God for one more step. Simply one step at a time. He only wants my trust in Him with my very next step. My very next step.

<u>Into His Word</u>

"Those who live in the shelter of the Most High will find rest in the shadow of the Almighty. This I declare of the LORD: He alone is my refuge, my place of safety; he is my God, and I am trusting him. "For he will rescue you from every trap and protect you from the fatal plague. He will shield you with his wings. He will shelter you with his feathers. His faithful promises are your armor and protection."
      Psalm 91:1-4 New Living Translation

"If you do what the LORD wants, he will make certain each step you take is sure. The LORD will hold your hand, and if you stumble, you still won't fall.
    Psalm 37:23-24 Contemporary English Version

A Brush and Paint

Yesterday afternoon on our way home from Tyler, we noticed a small, older house with part of its shingles removed and some new paint on one side. The house wasn't anything special; it looked just like many others around it.

As I turned my attention back to the highway, it was as if a voice inside of me said, "That house is just like each of you. Every person is under construction and remodeling......by God."

The voice continued, "During remodeling, though, you must practice two gifts from the Lord: patience and confidence. In every relationship you have, remember that God is working on those with whom you come in contact. With them, you must always practice Patience. He knows what they need.

"On the other hand, when you worry about doing or saying the wrong thing......or not doing things you know you should be doing......and you think that maybe God is just not around.....He still is. He will never leave you. You must have Confidence that He is actively at work within you..... remodeling."

The more I thought about it the more sense it made to me. God is not like some house painter or roofer who goes from job to job. He is the Great Transformer, working on each one of us. Some don't care, some have given up, some realize it, and some want more. His work in each of us here on earth.... never ends.

As a co-laborer with Christ, we each share the responsibility to be available ......to let Him onto our property....into the treasure room of our heart. Only then can He do the needed work where it makes the most difference.

Almost anyone can pick up a brush and paint the outside of a house, but only God can remodel any of us.......on the inside.

Into His Word

"Being confident of this very thing, that He who has begun a good work in you will complete it until the day of Jesus Christ;"
Philippians 1:6 New King James Version

"God has said, 'Never will I leave you; never will I forsake you.' So we say with confidence, The Lord is my helper; I will not be afraid. What can man do to me?"
Hebrews 13:5-6 New International Version

My Thoughts _____

_____

_____

_____

_____

Disconnected

For the past day or so I have really been frustrated with my printer, even though I know something about computers. To solve this problem, I tried my best to get it to print. I have done everything I knew how to do. This morning I even uninstalled the drivers, then reinstalled it all from the CD.

When the instructions offered 'Help' I skipped it....it is for people who don't know much about how to do this. I have been around computers for years. Again it didn't work.

I tried reinstalling one more time, but I did use 'Help'. My screen read "Unable to locate a printer." Reluctantly I crawled under my desk to check the back of the computer....wow! The cable was unplugged. All that wasted time, effort, frustration and worry.

All this time the printer was disconnected from its source. You see, they are machines made to communicate with each other. No connection, therefore no communication.

We do the same thing in our own lives, don't' we? We look at our problems from our own point of view, our own way of understanding? We try to solve them ourselves. We try to make things happen. We try everything but the right thing. We usually blame someone else...or we end up piling the blame on ourselves.

We look everywhere for the answers except the source. We don't realize that most likely we are simply disconnected. We have either lost contact with God or perhaps we never got plugged in, so to speak. He is who we are to communicate with daily. Again, no connection; no communication.

How come we are supposed to communicate with God? Well, He created us for fellowship with Him and created us in His image. His fingerprint is indelibly on us from day one. Our whole life we have God whispering in our ear, calling our name, calling us to Him...wanting our fellowship. He is wanting us to totally plug into Him....as our source.

Disconnected or partially plugged in; neither way will work for my printer. Without power or partially plugged in my printer is only an empty machine of no use. Without communication with God, I have no life, no future. I am only an empty body with no faith.....no love. But we have hope!

'Help' for our lives is the Word of God. There is a big difference with God, though. When we pray and believe Him for an answer, we really do get help!

Father, thank you that my printer became unplugged. I needed to remember about the connection between You and me. Actually, you have already promised better than just being connected. Your Son promised me that if I would simply accept Him, I would be grafted in instead.

                    Lord, I love you.........Warren

Into His Word

[Jesus said] I am the vine; you are the branches. If a man remains in me and I in him, he will bear much fruit; apart from me you can do nothing."
                John 15:4-5 New International Version

Their Votes Don't Count

A very good man, a close friend of ours, was just defeated in his bid for re-election to a public office here in Henderson. What the opposition said about him doesn't really matter, because enough people voted against him to remove him from office. That's the way it is in an election; some like you, some don't.

Isn't it great that other people's opinions and votes don't count with God? Really, if God listened to all the junk that someone else said about how a person lives his or her life, well, no one would ever 'get elected' or remain 'in office' as a child of God. God Himself decides......and ignores other people's votes.

When you disappoint your family or someone you love..... their votes don't count.

When you don't live up to others' expectations....their votes don't count.

When others in church don't like the clothes you wear or the way you worship....their votes don't count.

When someone else says all manner of things against you because you have a tattoo or your hair looks strange....... their votes don't count.

The only thing that counts with God is your personal acceptance of His Son into your heart and your life. Do you believe that Jesus Christ really died on the cross, for your sin, and was resurrected to eternal life.....as the Only Way for you to become a Christian and have eternal fellowship with the God of all creation? That counts with God.

It is when you have been drawn by the Holy Spirit into that personal decision to follow Christ that you know you were chosen by God to be His before the world began. He already knew about your failures, lies, cheating, adultery, and everything. He knew about what others say against you, whether those things are truth or lies.....and those votes don't count.

When you come to the place that you realize you cannot go on.....when you cannot make it through this life without Jesus as your Savior and Lord......when you accept the love that God has for you.....when you return that love to God and share it with others..... that is what counts.

Oh yeah, about our friend in county office? He is praising the Lord and seeking the heart of God for what God wants him to do next. After all, it is written, "If God be for me, who can be against me."

As for what the other people think of you, well, just remember: with God, their votes don't count.

Into His Word

"Praise be to the God and Father of our Lord Jesus Christ, who has blessed us in the heavenly realms with every spiritual blessing in Christ. For he chose us in him before the creation of the world to be holy and blameless in his sight."
                        Ephesians 1:3, 4 New International Version

"If God is for us, who can be against us?"
                        Romans 8:31 New International Version

Fillin' Up the Water Bowls

Mary Beth just got through reading me an email about "How to Know if you are a True Southerner." It had some very funny lines, but as I listened, one phrase about dogs brought to mind something that happened yesterday as I filled the water bowls for our dogs.

We try to keep all three bowls of water for Bailey and Delilah clean and free of any dirt or debris from the trees. Mary Beth has trained me well, as most of the time I empty each bowl, rinse it out, and then refill it with clean tap water. [I keep telling her the dogs will drink it anyway.] Sometimes, though, it is simply easier to use the sprayer attached to the end of the hose, setting it on "Full" so the bowls will fill faster.

Yesterday there was a leaf in the bottom of one bowl, so I changed the spray nozzle to "Jet" increasing the flow so it would overflow the bowl with such force that the leaf would come to the surface and float out over the top, thereby accomplishing the same thing as cleaning it….and it did.

It got me to thinking though, how many times God wants me to take the needed steps to get some sin out of my life – letting Him clean me up. Instead, I fight Him on it……letting the waters of His love swirl around me, but all the while I hold on to whatever the leaf in that bowl represents in my life.

Sometimes God uses His holy hand to clean us out and gently moves our hearts to respond to His Holy Spirit. On the other hand, I believe there are many times He increases the pressures in our lives, through circumstances like tough decisions we have to make, or by situations in our family life that arise, so that we will give Him the attention He desires and deserves.

In some cases God may use something that happens to us......like a car accident for example......to get us to sit up and pay more attention to the spiritual battles around us. Circumstances will remain out-of-sorts until we get rid of the things in our life that He does not want there. If we continue to ignore them, we face the rest of our life like a pot of simmering water......sometimes boiling over.....but never cooling down, either.

Please remember that no matter what happens to one of His children, God always desires His best for them. Every little thing that comes into the life of a believer, God uses for good.......no matter what we may think at the time.

When things around you seem chaotic and out-of-control, ask God what is going on....and what He is trying to teach you. Have confidence that nothing is ever wasted in His plans for your life.

Into His Word

"Wash me clean from all of my sin and guilt. I know about my sins and I cannot forget my terrible guilt.......Create pure thoughts in me and make me faithful again. Don't chase me away from you or take your Holy Spirit away from me. Make me as happy as you did when you saved me; make me want to obey!"
        Psalms 51: 2-3, 10-12 Contemporary English Version

Create in me a clean heart, O God........

Trapped!

Note: Delilah is our wonderful puppy and in this story when we mention her thinking and believing, we're simply sharing a story from our daily lives. We are not discussing whether beloved pets can have human thoughts or not. Please give us a little leeway in this, okay?

Delilah and I play a game. I pretend to try to get her and she goes from whining, to barking, to prancing, to dancing, all the while wagging her tail. When I slowly chase her around and around through different rooms, she runs away, and then comes back searching for me when I suddenly disappear into a closet or behind some furniture.

Today I rolled towards her in my computer chair, backing her into the sunroom. The door to the porch was closed and there I sat in my chair, blocking the only other exit. Delilah believed that I had her where she had no way to escape from my grasp.

She thought she was trapped. Usually when this happens in other parts of our home, (it's part of our game), she comes over to me very slowly and licks my hand as a gesture of giving up so she then can get out of the situation she's in.

I rolled my chair back and forth in the doorway, making noise on our wooden floor. She knew she couldn't get by my chair because the doorway is narrow and I would be able to reach out and touch her if she tried to run by me. She felt trapped!

The truth is that she was already safe from anything I wanted to do to her. My chair is too wide for that doorway. I wanted to go in, but I couldn't. No matter how badly I wanted to get

A Dirty Sink, A Bug, and Squirrels: God Speaks

to her......I couldn't. She didn't know that, though.

Even with all the noise I made and how threatening I appeared to Delilah, I still couldn't do anything but stay at the entrance. The truth is......she was safe as long as she stayed inside that room.

Many times you and I think that we are trapped in a similar situation with Satan blocking our door, making all kinds of noise about the things he is going to do to us. We mistakenly think there is no other way out, so we agree to a temporary compromise, lowering our standards of morality and decency down to his level. We tell ourselves it's okay, though, because "there was no other way," "I couldn't help myself," or "it was only that one time; it will never happen again." How wrong we are!

Satan knows he cannot enter a room where Christ dwells. When we are in Christ, we never have to accept Satan's offerings to us. When we do, it's because we think we have no other choice.

The real truth is that God always has His answer for our every situation.......no matter how bad it looks to us. He will never let us get so backed into a corner that He doesn't also offer an escape.

When I was at the door and Delilah was in the sunroom, all I had to do was make her think she was trapped, and then I had her doing what I wanted. In the same way, Satan cannot force us to do his bidding; he just has to convince us that his way is the only way out. But that is never the case.

Too many times we are fooled into believing that our

situation is desperate…….and *we must do something* to escape. We mistakenly think that the only doorway to freedom is blocked……when as a child of God we are already free.

We who are in Christ are safe in God's secure hands if we will just stay where He has us and choose from what our loving Father offers us. He loves us and His grace is always sufficient for our every need.

Because of the grace of God……..we are really never trapped!

Into His Word

"Cast all your anxiety on him because he cares for you. Be self-controlled and alert. Your enemy the devil prowls around like a roaring lion looking for someone to devour. Resist him, standing firm in the faith…...".
                    1 Peter 5:7-9a The New International Version

My Thoughts _____

_____

_____

_____

Between the Biscuit and Me

Mary Beth made some biscuits for our breakfast this morning so they just naturally looked up at me from my plate and cried, "Give us some honey, please!" They were so pitiful, lying on their backs, waiting. Of course I had to do what I could to ease their pain; I'm just that kind of guy.

I had the answer. Last week when Joy was in from San Antonio, the three of us stopped at a roadside stand over near White Oak, and I got some fresh local honey. A spoonful of the honey was held over my biscuits and the honey poured like, well, it poured like honey onto the biscuits one-at-a-time, filling up the little crater on top of each biscuit. Filled each one I did; almost to overflowing.

But then something happened that surprised me a little. One biscuit was near the outer edge of the plate, and since that part slants a lot, just a little of the honey had a chance to soak into the biscuit---most of it simply ran off the top, over the side, and down onto the plate....wasted. The biscuit was just not in a position to absorb the honey I poured over it.

A big difference between the biscuit and me is that the biscuit has no control over its position. It has to stay where I put it. It's just something Mary Beth made.....it has no life. I can pick up my biscuit from my plate, move it to a more level place, and force the honey into it. Then everything I have for it.....the biscuit absorbs. Nothing is wasted.

However, you and I are created by God. We are living, breathing human beings. He has given us the ability, the responsibility, to pick and choose from everything around us,

A Dirty Sink, A Bug, and Squirrels: God Speaks

daily deciding for ourselves what to accept, what to reject, and what to believe. And when we want to accept just part of something.....well, we do that, too.

There have been times in my own life that I have felt just like that biscuit. There was a part of me that just seemed empty. I mean, God was there, but somehow I was missing something that He had for me.

If I were a biscuit, God would have simply picked me up, put me where He wanted me, and made me do what He wanted. But God doesn't work that way. We're not biscuits.

God loves us, but He will not force His love down into us like honey into a biscuit. He will not make us accept anything He has for us; our decisions are ours alone.

What God has for us is a little like honey in that He is pours it over us. He is the only never-ending source of all that is good, but it is our choice of how much of Him we keep in our lives. For instance, there have been times that I felt like I just wasn't ready to listen to God or to receive what He had for me, so I didn't.

Other times, deep down inside, I knew I needed more of Him, but I just sat there telling God, okay, if you want me to have more.....then you make the change occur in me. You have to do it. Until then, I'll just sit here and wait....like some biscuit.

At breakfast, I said those biscuits cried out for honey, but I was only pretending. When you and I call upon the Lord, pretending just doesn't get it. Doing it just for show doesn't either. God knows when we are serious about Him.

When we are ready to build a new relationship with Him, or to deepen the one we already have with our Lord, then He will then pour more and more of Himself over us.....His way.....the only way....and none of it will ever be wasted.

No amount of honey on any number of biscuits can ever match that.

Into His Word

"How sweet are your words to my taste; they are sweeter than honey. Your commandments give me understanding; no wonder I hate every false way of life."
     Psalm 119:104-105 The New Living Translation

"May the God of your hope so fill you with all joy and peace in believing [through the experience of your faith] that by the power of the Holy Spirit you may abound and be overflowing (bubbling over) with hope."
     Romans 15:13 The Amplified Bible

"The Lord is righteous in everything he does; he is filled with kindness. The Lord is close to all who call on him, yes, to all who call on him sincerely. He fulfills the desires of those who fear him; he hears their cries for help and rescues them."
     Psalm 145:17-19 The New Living Translation

"The fear of the Lord is pure, enduring forever. The ordinances of the Lord are sure and altogether righteous. They are more precious than gold, than much pure gold; they are sweeter than honey, than honey from the comb."
     Psalm 19:9-10 The New International Version

Are You Being Friendly or Are You Married?

The sign saying "Puppies for Sale" is still out in front of our home advertising the remaining four DalmaDane puppies. Rays of sunshine are piercing the overcast skies just enough to allow me to write this morning.

Next door, our neighbor's front door swings open and Kay Castenada heads out to get something from their van. As she turns to go back inside, we both wave a good morning to each other. That's Henderson, Texas for you......being friendly.

Inside our home, Mary Beth is puttering around in our kitchen, waiting for some of our visiting children to come downstairs. She and I are much more than just friendly with one another.....we are married! Ours is a lifelong commitment sealed by God for loving, honoring, encouraging, cherishing, [all the warm and fuzzy stuff, of course].....and upholding each other above everyone else.

Being married is like what God wants with each of us. Unfortunately, many people treat Him only in a friendly way.....speaking to Him in passing.....or going to Him like someone asking their neighbor for a cup of sugar. Our Father wants more than just a simple wave and a good morning now and then.

God loves each one of us and desires to be our forever faithful partner in every thing we say and all we do. His rightful place in our life is above even our wife or husband, parents, or our children.

When we are more than just friendly with God, when we let God be Lord of our life......when we bond with Him like in a marriage......then and only then are we on the road to becoming what He desires for us to be.........deeply committed to loving Him.

Into His Word

"You cannot be my disciple, unless you love me more than you love your father and mother, your wife and children, and your brothers and sisters. You cannot come with me unless you love me more than you love your own life."
Luke 14:26 Contemporary English Version

"Love God, all you saints; God takes care of all who stay close to him, but he pays back in full those arrogant enough to go it alone."
Psalm 31:23 The Message

"This is how we know we're living steadily and deeply in him, and he in us: He's given us life from his life, from his very own Spirit. Also, we've seen for ourselves and continue to state openly that the Father sent his Son as Savior of the world."
1 John 4:13-14 The Message

Come Here, Delilah

Mary Beth is across the room grading test papers from her first Math exam of the semester. Delilah, our dog [who Mary Beth still calls her "puppy" although the Delilah is about 18 months old and weighs 45 pounds] is curled up on the little star-spangled-banner rug at her feet.

Mary Beth already had Delilah before she and I were married last year, so Delilah is still more at ease with her than with me. Delilah and I play around a lot, but it is a lot of me pretending to chase her, and she runs to another room, then comes back to see why I have not chased her. She and I enjoy barking at each other [that's the dog, not Mary Beth], hiding around corners and sneaking up on one another. When she doesn't know where I am, she either whines or she goes to find Mary Beth and stays close to her.

Just a few minutes ago, I sat in my chair and tried to get Delilah to come over to me. I held my hand out to her, but she just looked at me as I gently called her name and tried my best to talk her. She sat up, then slowly walked over to within a couple of feet, gave my hand a closer look, decided I did not have anything for her, so she returned to what she was doing over next to Mary Beth.

I was not trying to give her something to eat, I simply wanted to touch her, pet her, scratch her back......to show her I loved her. Please understand, I have never hurt her in any way, yet she still hesitates. Rarely is the time that she will come to me unless she wants something from me....like some food or a treat.

Unfortunately, that's the same way many people treat God. What I mean is, there are people who do not take a regular time every day just to be with God....in prayer, or quietness, or reading scripture....or anything.

They are the ones who know God.....only as a supplier....a giver. They use Him....only for what He can do for them. God hears from them when emergencies arise or they need money or some other kind of help. Jesus is not their personal friend.....not their counselor....not their Lord....and maybe not even recognized as their savior.

Usually these people do not want an *ongoing relationship*. They treat God like He is their sugar daddy....but certainly not as their Father.

And just like our dog, Delilah, they will get what they can.....then go back to the same thing they were doing before. They'll wait until their next need comes up....and then back to God they will go. They really just don't get it, do they? They are missing so much. So very much.

My Thoughts _____

_____

_____

_____

There Is No Life in the Fence

Our son, Crash, has moved in with us, bringing Bailey, his new Mom Dalmatian and her 10 puppies. Right now the pups are limited to the huge bed-like box he built for them. They are so cute; they just opened their eyes. So, it is with little bitty yelping in the background, that we are blessed with another joyous morning.

Most of us have been taught that God can be seen in everything around us. Today His handiwork is drawing my gaze to what is growing on the chain link fence we share with George and Kay. There are four or five kinds of ivy and creeping things growing with one another, stretching and climbing. We can learn something from a simple vine about our personal relationship with the Father.

For instance, if I were a vine, I would want to grow to be all that God has intended for me. As my leaves, my blooms, and my vines spread out all over the fence, I would strive to remember that all life is really in Him only. What good would it do for me to hold on so tightly to the fence that my roots get ignored? We've all seen vines like that, haven't we? They wither and die. There is no life in the fence itself, and I must never forget it.

What really counts is where I am rooted, not those things around me. As a vine, my blooms and how I weave my way up the fence get all the attention. As a believer, my value to God is the depth of my dependence upon Him, the depth of my conviction, and the love I have for Him and for others. In other words, to be like the real Vine, His son, Jesus.

A Dirty Sink, A Bug, and Squirrels: God Speaks

Although I was planted at the bottom of this fence that does not ensure that my vine will prosper. You see, in the plant world, the nutrients never move through the soil towards the roots that seek them. Instead, the roots move continuously..... .... searching wider and deeper for the richness within the soil where the vine is planted.

As a believer I want to remain rooted and grounded in Christ, bearing His fruit. And, as any good plant would tell you (if a plant could talk), this requires a dedicated root system......roots that want to feed on only the very best plant food...in my case, His Word.

To do this takes a hunger to grow daily beyond where I have before, seeking more of the Lord than I have ever known. For if the day comes when I am content to be just as I am, my roots will begin to draw in, I will cease to grow, and instead I will begin to die, eventually withering.

As for me, I need nothing outside of our Lord. Everything I seek is in the depths of the soil of His spirit. *But I have to do my part.* Just like the roots of the ivy plant, *I cannot simply sit by and say,* "Well, Lord, IF you want me to have a deeper relationship with you, make it happen. I've already tried. Now it's your turn. You come to me."

Life does not work like that, not in the plant world and not in our relationships with our Father. We must seek His face, His strength and His guidance every day, otherwise we are simply lost vines on the fence, going whatever way those around will let us go. He promises that the treasures of His Word are never buried beyond what our searching hearts can hope for or that our roots can reach.

A Dirty Sink, A Bug, and Squirrels: God Speaks

And I thought that was merely an ivy vine hanging across out driveway over there on our fence. It had 'message from God' written all over it.

Into His Word

"And I pray that you, being rooted and established in love, may have power, together with all the saints, to grasp how wide and long and high and deep is the love of Christ, and to know this love that surpasses knowledge--that you may be filled to the measure of all the fullness of God."
　　　　Ephesians 3:17-19 New International Version

"Now listen! A farmer went out to scatter seed in a field. While the farmer was scattering the seed, some of it fell along the road and was eaten by birds. Other seeds fell on thin, rocky ground and quickly started growing because the soil wasn't very deep. But when the sun came up, the plants were scorched and dried up, because they did not have enough roots. Some other seeds fell where thornbushes grew up and choked out the plants. So they did not produce any grain. But a few seeds did fall on good ground where the plants grew and produced thirty or sixty or even a hundred times as much as was scattered.
　　　　Mark 4:3-8 Contemporary English Version

"If anyone does not remain in me, he is like a branch that is thrown away and withers; such branches are picked up, thrown into the fire and burned.
　　　　John 15:6 New International Version

My Thoughts _____

_____

_____

In a Dog's Body

It was a little before seven this morning and Mary Beth was searching the sunroom for a cookbook that has a certain Banana Muffin recipe in it. As I walked down the hallway to add my two cents as to the hiding place of the book, I paused at the doorway leading to the living room, leaned up against the door frame, and looked towards the overstuffed chair next to the front windows.

There sat Delilah, still the puppy at almost two years old now. When I stopped and looked at her, her ears perked up and she somewhat froze from what she was doing. Although she is allowed in the house, Delilah is not permitted up on any of the furniture, yet there she sat, Queen of the Chair.

Well, she didn't move and neither did I. After a minute or so, she went back to chewing on her foot. Since I did not make her get down immediately, she probably took that as my approval of her disobedience.

I shuffled my foot on our wooden floor, making just enough noise to attract Delilah's attention. She sat upright and prepared to jump down. When once again I didn't do anything, she returned to enjoying her 'new-found Freedom' to do what she wanted. I simply smiled at her actions.

But as I watched her, the Lord was speaking to me and I began writing this piece in my mind. He loves me way too much to waste this experience. Just about then is when Mary Beth cried out in success; she had found the book and was going to use those bananas before they were past the eating stage.

A Dirty Sink, A Bug, and Squirrels: God Speaks

Seeing me leaning up against the doorway, she asked if I was okay. I said yes, and told her that God was teaching me something.

Delilah knew she was where she did not belong (as I sometimes find myself). She saw me and started to jump down (just like I do when I know I am in a situation that the Lord does not want me in), but when I did not move to make Delilah obey (like God does not make me obey Him), she just kept on doing what she had been doing (like I unfortunately do sometimes, also). She mistook my patience for my approval........the same way I do with the Lord occasionally.

You and I know when we are doing those things that God does not want us to do. He is not going to stop in the doorway, stare at us, and call down some hailstorm on us in order to make us do His will.

Instead, He sends His Holy Spirit continually, consistently, moment-by-moment to speak to our spirit about the love, forgiveness, and grace of our Lord........leading us into a deeper knowledge and understanding of the right things to do.......if we will just follow Him.

It was not Delilah ....it was really me, in a dog's body...... curled up in that chair in disobedience.

Please forgive me, Lord; I'd like to get down now. Please help me resist the temptation to get back up into places where I know you don't want me.

Into His Word

"Jesus answered and said to him, 'If anyone loves Me, he will keep My word; and My Father will love him, and We will come to him and make Our home with him. He who does not love Me does not keep My words; and the word which you hear is not Mine but the Father's who sent Me.

"These things I have spoken to you while being present with you. But the Helper, the Holy Spirit, whom the Father will send in My name, He will teach you all things, and bring to your remembrance all things that I said to you.'"
John 14:23-26 New King James Version

My Thoughts _____

_____

_____

_____

_____

It's Not Always Opportunity

Our conversation was interrupted by the pecking noise of the woodpecker about 25 feet away from where Mary Beth and I sat eating our early lunch. We had returned home from Common Ground worship and decided to enjoy our food outside on the patio.

The talk then turned to why a woodpecker has to make so much noise when looking for food. Supposedly, by pecking on the surface of the wood, the bird's noise brings the insects to the surface to see who is knocking at their door. When the little critters come out to see what's in it for them, the woodpecker devours them.

Those insects are more numerous in old posts, poles, and in dead or dying trees....things that have no life. That accounts for the louder noises, usually, because the sound of the woodpecker pecking tends to echo more in hollow places.

That's like Satan does things many times, too. He frequently finds people who are dead or dying spiritually and knocks, offering some opportunity for the unsuspecting person. Upon answering the knock, one looks at what is being offered and before one knows it, just like the woodpecker, Satan wounds or devours whoever answers.

Sometimes the woodpecker has to knock loudly and lots of times before any insects come out of the safety of where they live. Other times, a simple tap-tap-tap will do it. As a rule, the more life in a tree, the more pecking it will take to find a victim.

Using the same technique, many times Satan will knock at the door harder and longer, especially if the person is a strongly committed believer. He does not give up. The Bible assures us "you will have temptation." It does not stop just because one is saved or joins a church. Will have temptation means will have temptation. Everyone will. No one is exempt – not even Jesus.

Our God always makes a way of escape. It is our responsibility to be in prayer and remember: That knocking.....well, it's not always opportunity.

Into His Word:

"Be self-controlled and alert. Your enemy the devil prowls around like a roaring lion looking for someone to devour."
      1 Peter 5:8 New International Version

"Dear brothers and sisters, whenever trouble comes your way, let it be an opportunity for joy. For when your faith is tested, your endurance has a chance to grow. So let it grow, for when your endurance is fully developed, you will be strong in character and ready for anything."
      James 1:2-4 New Living Translation

"This shows that the Lord knows how to rescue godly people from their sufferings and to punish evil people while they wait for the day of judgment."

    2 Peter 2:9 Contemporary English Version

A Tree on the Next Island

There is a very beautiful tree on the next island over from me. From where I am, I can make out the wonderful different shades of green and its very oval shape.

One would think that the tree would be noticed by everyone. Most people, though, going their own way, seem to merely take it for granted.

In the same way, many of us simply pass by beautiful people in our lives every day. According to the world value system, beauty means beauty to the eye.

Real beauty, however, is found inside of a person. It is defined by a kind, gentle spirit that is more interested in doing for others. It is a life motivated by putting self last......not first.

Inner beauty is birthed inside......love deposited by God deep in the rich soil of one's heart. The season of growth for that seed is different from one person to another, too.

Like that tree on the next island, these beautiful people are often overlooked. By nature, they tend to 'blend-in' by putting other's feelings and needs above their own and drawing no attention to themselves.

The next island is actually a concrete island here in a Lowe's parking lot where I sit in our car waiting for Mary Beth and Crash to return from shopping. It is not some South Pacific island paradise.

We must want to find beauty before we can really see it and many times we find it where we least expect to find it. If we look deep enough, we can discover some good and some beauty in every person we pass in life.

And that tree on the next island......well, that tree could be you......simply not seen or appreciated by others......yet. Be patient. In the meantime, remember this: You ARE loved.

My Thoughts _____

_____

_____

_____

_____

I Wanna Be a Cloud

If you were looking for us last Tuesday night around 10:00, we were dancing on a deserted shore at Lake Tyler. We had been driving home from dinner, celebrating our 2nd wedding anniversary, when, as we crossed the bridge on Hwy 64, the beauty of the lake beckoned us and we just could not resist.

The only other car was parked near the boat ramp in the little park, and its owners were apparently out fishing. Since the wind had already gone to bed, the surface of the lake was like glass. I went around, opened Mary Beth's door and invited her to step outside the car to dance.

We did, too, out in the middle of a parking lot, in the dark of night, and not to any man-made tune. We danced to that special music that plays deep inside two people who have been joined into one with their Lord.

Although it was a cloudy night, we could easily see each other. There were not any lights in the immediate area, either. In fact, we were surprised that we could make out lots of things around us.

We realized that we were being blessed by the glow from the low-hanging clouds overhead. The clouds extended to the city lights of Tyler, almost 5 miles away, and that glow just naturally spread through the clouds all the way out to where we were. The city lights were helping the country couple dance.

With a sweep of His marvelous brush, God's artwork on the canvas of His sky was a masterpiece of how each one of us is to be with Him. We are to be His works of art for all to see and we are to remain so close to Him that the glow of His light, His radiance, brings light to others. This is our privilege, our blessing, our calling by being His children.

As Mary Beth said to me that night, "I wanna be a cloud." And I replied, "Me, too."

My Thoughts _____

_____

_____

_____

_____

Not a Night Light, Please

In our bathroom......there lives a little night light. It's one of those kinds that has a sensor built into it so that whenever it is dark, the light comes on automatically. It even comes on in the daylight hours, though. Just yesterday when I was brushing my teeth, I leaned over the sink, blocking off the outside light from the window. When the shadow of my body blocked the light's sensor, 'Hello, here's your light!' It came on.

When the sensor receives any light from the outside, it is almost always from the sun. And that light, even when it is just a glow, is brighter than that little night light bulb. So when it senses any light......it does not have to work at all. The light simply sits there. Its sensor tells the night light, "What you are receiving is much more powerful and brighter than anything you can produce yourself."

The night light by itself produces barely enough of a glow for one's eyes to simply see images......nothing more. One cannot shave by it, or put on makeup, or clean out a cut or a wound. Things become a little vague. Some things become distorted. The night light comes on......ONLY when something comes between it and the light. The sensor believes there is no light, therefore it thinks it has to produce some.

So how much am I really like that night light? When something comes between the Light of the Lord and me, even those things over which I have no control, whether it brings just a shadow or even total darkness, how often do I try to turn on my own little light? In other words, how often do I try to live my life running on my own power instead of being dependent upon God?

Most of the time, though, when there is darkness, whether I am aware of it or not, it is because of my own choices......my own decisions. In most of those cases, I don't even know I'm trying to run on only ME!

It is a great temptation for me to try to produce on my own, when the Bible says that my best is just a pile of filthy rags. Darkness! My fault or not. On my own, I can do nothing.

Lord God, I come before You today destitute in who I am without you. Most of the time I come willingly, yet there are many times that I leave scratch marks on the floor while being drawn by Your Holy Spirit into Your throne room. It's like I just can't let go of some of the little things that come between You and me.

And yet, when I am in Your presence, none other has a chance of diverting my eyes from You or misdirecting my actions. My heart is filled with gladness and overwhelming joy.

I know that no matter what I bring before You from this world in which I live, it is all meaningless when compared to what You offer to me every day of my life. There is no amount of money I can give, no number of hours I can work in any church or ministry, no dedication or commitment I can make on my own, which would shine any more than a night light would on the outside of my home in the direct light of the sun.

Thank you, Lord, that the Light of Your Word exposes the weakness and frailty of what I think is the best I can do. My inward, deepest desire is that there be no shadows between us. Let the sensor in my heart always be grounded in Your promises for my life and may the current of Your love forever flow through my words, my thoughts, and my actions.

A Squirrel is on Our Cable

A most excellent morning is this. It is 6:30 on January 2, 2004, and it is wonderful outside in our backyard. The Hughby-Dughby thermometer shows an unbelievable 68 degrees in the middle of winter. Wow! What a way to start the day.

Back towards the garden, the COCH [that's cut-out-cow's head] peeks around the tree to see what I am doing out so early. Puppy Delilah has one of our granddogs in for a visit, and they are chasing each other wildly around the yard. A couple of squirrels are playing tag in the trees overhead, leaping from limb to limb as they frolic about.

Outlined against the dawn of many colors, doing a balancing act as it makes its way from one corner of the property to another, a solitary squirrel is on our cable wire, going from power pole to power pole. When the dogs spot this squirrel, they suddenly set aside play time and give all their attention to it.

They run over beneath the wire and look up as if to say, "Hey, we hope you slip. And we're gonna eat you up when you do." [They talk like this because they are both good East Texas dogs.] Slowly they move closer and closer to their suspected prey......waiting for just one little slip.

This movement by Delilah and Rocky gets the squirrel's attention and it stops on mid-wire. Close, but not close enough to matter, so the squirrel continues its run on the wire until it reaches the other side.

Such a chance those squirrels take in running that wire. I saw one fall off one day, but Delilah was either resting or inside the house, so all that happened was the squirrel hit the ground with a bounce, and was off running for its life....even though no danger was in sight and there was nothing around to harm it.

How about you and me? Do we have a cable wire, too? What kind of unnecessary chances do we take? Are we like that squirrel, looking around to see who's watching before we do something we shouldn't be doing?

If your situation is like mine and most people's, you do things like that. That squirrel could have taken the safer route, but chose to use the cable wire instead. Squirrels don't have the thought process you and I do, so most likely it uses the wire out of habit. You and I decide to take our own chances on purpose.

Many times we behave like we think Satan has gone inside the house or that he is on the other side of the yard, resting and that should we make a slip, a wrong decision, or a little mistake, he will simply miss it and nothing will happen to us. The truth is that we are promised Satan is just like a roaring lion, prowling about, seeking whom he may devour. That does not say he will simply scratch us. It says devour.

It is his job......to lie, to steal and to destroy. That is, to devour our thoughts, steal the love and adoration we have for the Lord, and to destroy all the light the Lord shines though our lives. Devour!

Yet many of us have arrived at a point that our attitudes towards the world are just as casual as that squirrel's. We are simply letting the world slowly, methodically move mountains of immorality deeper into our lives and we are more and more living these lower levels of morality as normal. We have become just like the squirrel, walking a very thin cable. Yes, very carefully at first, but then, the more we run on that cable, the more acceptable and casual we become about the wrong things in our lives.

Satan is here for the stragglers, those of us who wander from the truth, even if only for a moment, maybe only in our own minds. His bait is the world. He assures us that his cables are safe to balance on; "Look over here, walk this way; nothing will happen. No one will know."

The squirrels will run again and again on our cable wire and hope that if they fall, the dogs will be in at rest in a far part of the yard or maybe inside the house. For you and me......Satan never rests......never goes inside......always pays attention for even the smallest action. He is prowling about......waiting for an opening......or our slip on the cable we shouldn't even be on in the first place.

Yet we continue taking chances......seeing how close to the edge we can get. We slide the ends of our toes closer and closer to the edge......thinking we are safe......because no one else will ever find out......that no one knows. We are wrong......because that wire we are on......well, it's in God's garden......and He knows.

The Water Is Always Hot

Mary Beth was already waiting for me in the car. I had just finished cleaning our car windows, though, and had some yucky stuff on my hands; I had to wash them off before we left for school.

The dishwasher was going, so I knew that the water at the faucet in the kitchen would get hot quickly. It was just matter of how fast it would get hot and if I could wash my hands before the water burned me.

I figured I could turn on the water, push the plunger on the little pink bottle to get soap, and wash my hands. That way I'd be through before the water could get too hot.

I tried….it did…..I didn't…..it did……….ouch! I lost. Sound familiar?

It's the same way most of us approach sin. We think we can get in, do what we want and get out of it before it hurts us. So we do, we can't, it does……..so it hurts over and over again. We always lose. Sin is not a competitive sport. It is for keeps.

The water is always hot at the faucet of temptation. Once we decide that we can do something wrong and not get burned, we've already lost.

Bailey and Delilah

We took Bailey and Delilah for a walk this morning. Delilah walked calmly along with us. However, Bailey constantly tugged and pulled me down the street, wanting to chase cats or squirrels, or get into someone else's garbage.

Bailey does not respond much to my voice. She is Crash's dog, and he has her very well 'voice trained.' She responds great to Crash's voice, but she is not used to mine.

When we are out walking together, she usually only responds when I tug on her leash. On a leash, she has to do what her master demands.

In His great wisdom, God does not have any of us on a leash. God desires our obedience, but does not force it upon us. When left to our own choices, we sometimes run off in all directions, looking for something, anything, to bring us temporary satisfaction……and we usually end up in the garbage.

In the meantime, both for now and for eternity, what our Father desires and has designed as best for each one of us is to walk beside Him listening intently to His voice……in obedience to His voice.

There is no leash for us……only freedom in Him.

Into His Word

"My sheep recognize my voice. I know them, and they follow me."
                                John 10:27 The Message

"There's far more here than meets the eye. The things we see now are here today, gone tomorrow. But the things we can't see now will last forever."
                        2 Corinthians 4:18   New International Version

"I'm all ears, all eyes before you......you're my only hope! Teach me how to live to please you, because you're my God."
                                Psalm 143:8-10 The Message

My Thoughts _____

_____

_____

_____

_____

How's Your Reception?

As I was driving from Henderson to Tyler this morning, I was talking to Mary Beth on my cellphone. Trees in varying shades of green majestically guard all 32 miles. The trip doesn't take that long, but it seems to pass ever more quickly when she is actually with me.

However, today she was busy being Susie Homemaker while I attended to errands in the big city, so we found ourselves talking by cellphone. At first we would have a clear signal, then our voices would be garbled....then she could hear me....then I couldn't hear her.

Our communication depended upon whether or not I received any signal. The signal varied with how far I was from the signal tower.....then whether I was in the midst of too many trees.....or on top of a hill. It is a little discouraging to lose the sound of her voice because something's wrong with our line of communication.

We've all been there.....time and time again. Perhaps right now you are in a place in your life where you are having a little trouble "receiving God's signals." Since God always hears you, and He always answers you when you call Him, what's between you and God that would keep you from hearing Him?

Maybe you have strayed too far from His tower, the Bible. Perhaps you can't make out what He is saying, or that you cannot recognize His voice because it's been a while since you spent much quality time with Him. You think you know His voice but you're not sure.

A Dirty Sink, A Bug, and Squirrels: God Speaks

When my cell signal has trouble, I go more out into the open or farther up a hill......and my reception gets better.

When we open up more to God and spend time with Him exploring the rich gardens of His Word......our reception of Him always improves, that is, we are always able to hear Him better. Isn't that what each of us really desires?

Into His Word

"Answer me when I call to you, O my righteous God. Give me relief from my distress; be merciful to me and hear my prayer."
        Psalm 4:1 New International Version

"To the LORD I cry aloud, and he answers me from his holy hill."
        Psalm 3:4 New International Version

"I call on the LORD in my distress, and he answers me."
        Psalm 120:16 New International Version

My Thoughts _____

_____

_____

_____

Throwing Away Cold Coffee

I just returned from walking around our block in that time of the morning that languishes between darkness and dawn. There was a chill in the air......cooler than I had anticipated. I had made a fresh pot of Caramel Truffle coffee earlier for Mary Beth (I make the coffee every morning for her....one of my little pleasures), so I took an insulated cup of it with me.

When I got back from my walk, I noticed my coffee had cooled down considerably more than I thought it would have, so the remainder of the coffee found its home on our front grass. I stood for a moment, arms propped up on the top of the chain-link fence, watching the colors of day make their way between our neighbor's trees and into that capsule of beauty we call dawn.

Throwing away my coffee triggered thoughts about how we do the same thing with our food. We push aside food just because it is not the right temperature. It's not the way we like it best, so we get rid of it, throw it way.

The food is still good in many cases.....vitamins and all that stuff, but so many of us throw it away just because it doesn't feel just right, or taste exactly the way we think it should. Something we like hot gets a little cool, or something we like real cold....well, maybe it becomes room temperature, so we decide to get rid of it.

That's how we mistakenly handle our spiritual life many times. We listen or don't listen, depending upon how the message hits our spiritual taste buds. Unfortunately we reject some sermon or message because of petty little things like the way someone is dressed, or even something as trivial as the way a person's wears his or her hair.

Even if it may not be what we really want to hear right then, it may be exactly what God wants us to hear.....even when it doesn't feel good to hear it. That message is like the taste of something we would rather set aside until another time, or in many cases, not hear at all.

We miss out on changes that God is trying to bring about in our lives, because we either don't or won't listen. We have a tendency to reject it because it doesn't feed us in a good touchy-feely way, or it is not done in exactly the way we would want to hear it, or it may be something we don't want to face, or it may expose a weakness in our armor.

Whatever it is, too many times our response is "Not right now. That's not important. You don't know what you're talking about."

Each of us has those whom the Lord has put into our lives who do love us enough.....who do care about us enough that they speak the truth even when we don't want to listen. Although the timing of tough love and Godly encouragement may not always be to our liking, we should praise Him for these people.

Our relationships with God and with those around us....well, they both take time and work....from all sides.

The Word of God promises that everything will always work for our good when we are called for His purpose. We should strive to not be too hasty to ignore something because it is not exactly perfect.

A Dirty Sink, A Bug, and Squirrels: God Speaks

We must not make the mistake of treating everything around us like cold coffee....don't automatically throw it away. God's message of hope and love are always just the right temperature....no matter what we may think.

My Thoughts _____

_____

_____

_____

What's Making You Dance Today?

A leaf is dancing across our driveway as I sit in our swing this morning. Crash got this swing for us and assembled it yesterday as a surprise. It was a very thoughtful thing to do. We love our swing.

That leaf and some of its friends are collectively dancing and twirling across the pavement about 20 feet away. They appear to be a cluster of confusion, unlike some new friends of ours who danced joyously together following supper last night at their house.

One of my students had invited us over to celebrate and share in their Sabbath dinner. It was a first time for us. The tradition, including each person there reading the Word of God, sharing the good food, and the on-going fellowship, was very heartwarming.

Unlike our friends, who danced voluntarily because they wanted to and because the Spirit of God in their hearts moved them to, the party of leaves in our driveway was being picked up, spun around and tossed by erratic little gusts of wind. Wherever the breeze bounced them, the leaves stayed.....waiting for whatever would happen next.

What a contrast between the leaves and our friends! Leaves with no choice of their own, sunning themselves on the clean pavement, next maybe getting stuck in the grass of our lawn, even being tossed into the street to be run over by car tires or crushed into trash by someone out for a stroll. Poor leaves.

On the other hand, our friends last night were led by the spirit of God, by what the Word and their tradition had passed down to them through the ages. Celebrating Yeshua (Jesus), they chose to dance.

Each one of us dances every day....*to some tune*.....played by someone or something. Whatever drives our dance is either something we sincerely believe that we have treasured deep down inside of us or it is simply circumstances; spur-of-the-moment happenings.

Whatever we let drive our dance......it is what we love. We choose our own music and we decide our partner.

Who are you dancing with today? Maybe not physically, but spiritually? Are your feet moving to the music from 'whoever plays', or is it your faith in God.....in His love and trustworthiness to take care of your every need?

Our prayer is that we can come into agreement with Joshua from the Old Testament, when, with a grateful heart, he said, "As for me and my house, we will serve the Lord."

Into His Word

"David, ceremonially dressed in priest's linen, danced with great abandon before GOD. The whole country was with him as he accompanied the Chest of GOD with shouts and trumpet blasts."
                              2 Samuel 6:14-15 The Message

"You can't worship two gods at once. Loving one god, you'll end up hating the other. Adoration of one feeds contempt for the other. You can't worship God and Money both."
                                      Matthew 6:24 The Message

The Grasp

I am in the backyard this morning, watching nature wake up. The Castenada's cats are sneaking through the grass or strutting around like they own the world. You cat owners know what I mean. On the other hand, dogs are barking at those cats to quit showing off and go away. I have my cup of coffee, and well, it is just wonderful in the swing.

What especially caught my attention a couple of moments ago was a robin that flew from the upper branches of our large pecan tree down to the smaller dogwood tree. As the bird leaned back and started to light, it lowered its feet and pulled them back, somewhat like an airplane landing gear would operate.

The bird readied its feet to firmly grasp what it saw as a secure branch. Over and over, day in and day out, that bird flies from place to place, out of instinct looking for what it believes is firm.....something to grasp that will keep it safe.

As I watched, I believe the Lord whispered to my spirit, "What you're seeing is an excellent picture of a person's walk through life. Deep down inside, everyone wants something that is safe to hold onto....something to grasp.

"One goes from decision to decision, either listening to Me or choosing for themselves, drifting from place to place, looking for something that looks firm to them. Humans are created higher than any dog, or cat, and, as in this case, a bird.

"Animals and birds have only instinct to guide them. People are the only ones I created in My image. Each of you have Me to look to for guidance. You make your choices out of what you believe. There is no security outside of Me."

In Jesus Christ there are no shaky limbs upon which to land. All of our hope, our love, our faith is in Him……in His grace. He is the Rock of our Salvation. He desires our all…….our every bit of trust is to be in Him alone.

Individually, we should ask ourselves, "Are the fingers of my heart and the hands of my mind always ready to grip and grasp His Word, or do I simply fly around in life, hoping that what I have hold of is strong enough to support me until I fly away looking for something else?"

There is only one answer, one foundation, one tree of eternal life whose branches will always be secure for us. That tree, that one vine of security………..the Savior of the world and the very best friend we'll ever have…..His name is Jesus.

My prayer and encouragement is this: Grasp His hand while the choice can still be made. No one stays in flight forever and any of us may have to land before we know it.

Into His Word

"I am the vine; you are the branches. If a man remains in me and I in him, he will bear much fruit; apart from me you can do nothing."
        John 15:5 New International Version

"I will show you what he is like who comes to me and hears my words and puts them into practice. He is like a man building a house, who dug down deep and laid the foundation on rock. When

a flood came, the torrent struck that house but could not shake it, because it was well built.
"But the one who hears my words and does not put them into practice is like a man who built a house on the ground without a foundation. The moment the torrent struck that house, it collapsed and its destruction was complete."
Luke 6:47-49 New International Version

"You're my cave to hide in, my cliff to climb. Be my safe leader, be my true mountain guide. Free me from hidden traps; I want to hide in you. I've put my life in your hands. You won't drop me, you'll never let me down."
Psalm 31:1-3 The Message

"The LORD is my rock, my fortress and my deliverer; my God is my rock, in whom I take refuge, my shield and the horn of my salvation. He is my stronghold, my refuge and my savior....from violent men you save me."
2 Sam 22:2-3 New International Version

My Thoughts _____

_____

_____

_____

_____

About Warren and Mary Beth, the Authors

x x x x x x x

Warren's Story

x x x x x x

What About This Jesus?

x x x x x x x

Alphabetical Listing of Stories

x x x x x x x

My Thoughts
(for making notes)

About Warren and Mary Beth, the Authors

Mary Beth and Warren both teach Math at Tyler Junior College in Tyler, Texas. In fact, they met during the fall semester of 2002. Their story was actually written up in the campus newspaper under the heading of "Love Finds a Way at Potter Hall."

After 20 years of hectic, metropolitan lifestyle, Mary Beth had inherited her parents' house in Henderson, allowing her to escape the wilds of big-city life in Dallas, and embrace small-town life in East Texas. A short 35-minute drive down a tree-lined highway put Mary Beth at her job and in perfect position for the next phase of God's plans for her life.

During the previous two years, God had saved Warren's life through miracle after miracle. Warren was just returning to teaching at TJC after a two-year absence when he was hired to assist Mary Beth in one of her Math classes. Wow, what a God-incidence!

Warren and Mary Beth were married March 8, 2003, in the backyard of Mary Beth's house, complete with doves cooing in the trees. Together they have six grown children: Shannon, Warren II, Joy, Jason (who goes by Crash), Matt, and Crystal. They also have five and a half grandchildren: Kenny, Zachary, Avery, Aedyn, Cade and soon-to-be-born Kaedynce.

They still live in the house in Henderson, along with their two very spoiled dogs, Coco and Delilah. (Who on earth names their dog Delilah? Well, when your old dog is named

Sampson, and you get a new female puppy, what else would you name her? Besides, Delilah sounds great in East Texan – "De-li-lah! Get yourself in this house!")

Life is good! Don't ya' think? As Mary Beth says, "We love our small town life!" And Warren agrees!

Warren's Story

"Jesus." The last word out of my mouth before impact in a head-on collision on Interstate 20 near Canton, Texas.

"Jesus." The first word out of my mouth when I woke up after a 48-day coma following that accident.

Thanksgiving Day 2000, I was on my way to visit my Mom in Fort Worth. A light drizzle was bathing the surface of the highway and as best as I can remember, I had my cruise set at around 50.

Just as I went under an overpass my little pickup truck began to hydroplane, turning my truck at a 45 degree angle. When my tires came in contact with the dry pavement under the overpass, the cruise took over, sending me in the direction I was now aimed......across the median strip.

I missed the overpass supports and I missed the guard rails, but my path took me across the slick, grassy median (which is only about 50 feet across at that point) into the oncoming traffic. At 50 miles per hour, it doesn't take long to cross 50 feet of grass. I know; I did it and by the grace of God, I lived.

There was no way to miss the van coming from the opposite direction. I looked at the van, at the driver, back at the van, and I spoke *His name*, *Jesus*. Not a scream. Not in panic. Just His name as a one word prayer.....then impact!

The pickup was on its side; my driver door was against the

highway. The impact had split the gas tank open, the fumes ignited, and immediately flames billowed like clouds from beneath the dashboard. Flames engulfed my seatbelt and I could not reach down to release the lock. I was awake, trapped, and on fire!

Seemingly from nowhere, three men appeared – one kicked in the front windshield for an escape route; another one used his knife to cut the seat belt and free me; and the third one used his handheld fire extinguisher to try to put out the flames that were burning my clothes from the lower part of my body.

The men pulled me out over the top of the steering wheel and when they had carried me about 15-20 feet, one of them asked me, "Is there anyone else in the vehicle?" The second I told them no, the truck exploded. Ten seconds longer and my rescuers and I would have all blown up in the fiery explosion, but that was not God's plan.....for them or for me either.

Nightmares filled almost all of the next 48 days and nights of my life in the coma. There was one time, however, that I vaguely recall two of my sons, Warren II and Crash, standing beside my bed. As best I could, I tried desperately to tell them about the nurses and others who I thought were part of the groups trying to kill me, or at least I thought I told them.

The massive medicines did wonders for me, but apparently did not help my thinking or my speech a lot. Even though I remember being very serious about what I was trying to tell them, neither son could make heads or tails from what I said.

Forty-eight days after the accident, January 9th of 2001, I opened my eyes and looked around. I remembered that I had been in the accident, but I thought it was the day before.

A Dirty Sink, A Bug, and Squirrels: God Speaks

I was alive!

I did not know where I was (LSU Burn Unit in Shreveport, thank you, Lord!), but I knew the first thing I had to do was to praise God for saving my life. I didn't have any idea how badly I was hurt and I couldn't move any part of my body, but I knew my life was spared only by the grace and love of our Lord Jesus Christ. I needed somehow to praise God.

I tried to remember the 23rd Psalm, but could only think of the first line or two. Next I tried to think through the Lord's Prayer, but again, could not remember much. Then I began to think about the name Jesus. Only Jesus. Not some formal, complicated, preachy prayer……simply the name above all names…..the only one worthy to be praised: Jesus.

As I mentioned, I couldn't move any part of my body, so the hot tears just rolled down my cheeks…..tears of happiness and joy that partner with giving praise to Almighty God. Then I stopped for a moment. I recalled that during a weekly Bible study group about six months earlier, we had discussed the difference between thinking things to God and speaking to Him out loud.

Especially in the New Testament, I believe we are taught that we should speak our praise to God aloud, not just think it in our minds. Since Satan cannot read our minds, and I wanted Satan to know that I was lifting praise to God for what had happened, I began to speak the name of Jesus out loud.

One of my nurses then noticed I was awake. It may have been the tears or maybe the noise I was making in my praise. (I didn't know it at the time, but I had tubes running into my lungs and my tongue was severely swollen from the coma.)

A Dirty Sink, A Bug, and Squirrels: God Speaks

Whatever I was saying probably was not understandable to the human ear. Even if my nurse couldn't understand my praise, my Father in Heaven surely could. He understands all languages.....known and unknown.....nothing misses His ears.

The doctors estimated that I would be hospitalized for about a year and in rehab for 2 years. Through God's healing power, I was released from the hospital in about 2 months and was in rehab for only 6 months. What a miracle worker He still is!

I discovered later that the doctors had told my family and friends that I would probably die in the coma---that I would most likely never wake up. They told me that if they had thought I would survive, they would have amputated my left leg at the knee and my right foot because both were so damaged I would never walk again. God had different plans, though. Praise His name!

The "big wreck" as Mary Beth and I call it, was the second of three accidents that I was in during a five year period. The first had occurred in March of 1997, three years previous. I was walking across the loop in Tyler when a car hit me. My broken pelvis required many months of recovery and a change of profession, from customer rep (salesman) to being a college student in order to learn a new career: computers.

I began attending Tyler Junior College in the fall of 1997, learning how to work with computers. After a couple of years of classes, however, I began to teach some computer lab classes part time for the college. By the fall of 2000, I was on full time faculty, and then came the big wreck. But teaching at TJC fit nicely into God's plans for my future as you will soon see.

A Dirty Sink, A Bug, and Squirrels: God Speaks

The third wreck happened about 6 months after being released from rehab from the big wreck. I got hit by another vehicle. My car had stalled on the way home one Saturday night about 11:30. I was only about a mile from home, so I decided to walk, but stayed way over in the grass, about 10 feet off the pavement.

It was a good idea, but the wrong distance. Not quite far enough off the road. Probably 10 feet, 7 inches would have been far enough, but that was not to be.

I was still recovering from the big wreck, but had graduated to living at home and walking with a cane. My left leg was still in a cast. As I walked in the grass alongside the two lane road in Chapel Hill, the driver of a truck from behind me was blinded by oncoming headlights and came off the road, hitting my left side with the truck's passenger mirror and sending me flying about 10 feet in the air into a grassy ditch.

As I watched the driver drive off into the night, once again I talked quickly to God. To the best of my knowledge, my side of the conversation went something like this: Lord, I know I'm hit really badly again. I'm ready to go, but I really want to stay. Please let me stay.

I saw the rear lights of the car suddenly brighten as the brakes were applied. The driver turned left into a driveway and turned around to come back. As the car approached, the only thing I could move was my left leg, the one still in the cast from the big wreck.

Since the grass was higher than my body, the driver didn't see me. I prayed more as the car went up to the top of the hill and I heard it turn around. I used my leg to move the grass around me and somehow the driver saw the movement, and pulled over to where I lay. A couple more cars followed the driver into the grass. I then prayed no one would run over me since they could not see me because of the grass.

The people who stopped didn't know our location, so I borrowed one of their cell phones and, as I lay in the ditch, I called 911. I knew exactly where we were. It was quite a shock to find out that I was connected to a 911 operator 300 miles away, near San Antonio. In fact, she did not even know where I was, even after I gave her the name of the town. She said I was 'out of her area', asked me to write down the 911 local number, and began to give me the number.

I firmly expressed my horrible condition and explained that I had been hit by a truck, that I was in a ditch, in the dark, had no pen or paper, and I needed an ambulance immediately. I asked her to please connect me to the Smith County 911. At this point, she thanked me for calling 911 and she hung up on me. I was not a really happy camper at that point.

I borrowed another cell phone, called 911, and got our Smith County office operator. The ambulance driver got lost on his way to pick me up. The highway patrolman did not, though, and he told the ambulance driver how to find us.

When asked why he came back, the driver of the truck that hit me told the highway patrolman that he thought he hit a deer and wanted to see what it looked like. Just between you and me, I know that God put that thought in his mind so he would come back to me.

You see, later I found out that the impact had exploded my spleen, broken my left ribs, and that I was in the process of bleeding to death internally......I just didn't know it at the time. 18 mg of Coumadin will make blood run like mercury, and it was doing it to mine.

If the driver of the truck had not come back, I would have bled to death in the grass, over in the dark, on a Saturday night, out in the country. But that was not in God's plans.

I was taken to ETMC Tyler in critical condition, again! The doctors helped save my life. They released me in 11 days, and I was walking again in about 2 weeks. God is still in the miracle working business......even though we certainly don't deserve it!

Another year later, and another miracle was waiting to happen in my life: I was about to meet Mary Beth!

The miracles were not because God considered me a moral, righteous person, for I was not. The amazing things that God pulled me through were not some kind of reward for doing the right things. Along with really hearing and obeying God, I made a number of wrong choices, too. And of course He knew all of this.

The Bible tells us that His ways are not our ways. For reasons I do not understand, He once again spared my life.

I did not deserve it then; I still don't. That's why God calls it grace.

A little more information:
In between the 1st accident and the crash-and-burn I-20 accident, Jean, my loving wife of 27 years was found to have cancer; the following year she passed away. She was a

beautiful person who gave our family many years of love, devotion, and kindness. She is missed.

And one last thing:
IF God were to take me back to Thanksgiving 2000, to the split second before impact on I-20, and offer me the choice of missing the van or crashing into it and burning, then I'd go through it all again........the coma, the nightmares, all the extended pain and getting hit the next year.......just to be able to know Him more and to experience His intense faithfulness, His overwhelming love, and His awesome grace all over again.

............warren

What About This Jesus?

As we wrote these stories, we also shared things that arose from our relationship with our Lord, Jesus Christ. Sometimes we called Him Lord, sometimes Savior, referred to him as Jesus, or the Christ. Maybe you're wondering about this Jesus yourself.

Is He real? And if He is real (and He definitely is!), then you may be asking yourself if this Jesus is for you. The Word of God promises an emphatic yes! The changed lives of tens of millions of people are testimonies to the love, the forgiveness, and the faithfulness of the Christ. God loves you and His Son, Jesus Christ loves you and wants a relationship with you......a personal one that is there for the asking.

When it comes to knowing Jesus, some people are mainly interested in being saved from Hell. That's kinda like being scared into doing something because you fear the 'what if you don't' consequences. Now, there's nothing wrong with that either. After all, without Christ, Hell is destination central.

Fear of Hell did not move me to ask Jesus into my heart. I (Warren) asked Jesus to be my Savior and Lord because I was tearing myself up inside. I needed help in the Here and Now.

On the surface my life looked okay to most people, but deep down inside, I was carrying around a bunch of garbage and I stunk spiritually. I needed a Jesus who would walk beside me that I could talk with about my problems and a Lord that would guide me down this path called life.

I was shown in the Bible that God created us to love Him and be dependent upon Him for our every decision. He sent His

Son, Jesus, to make it possible for us to have continuous contact with Him. That is what I needed. That is what I received. In Jesus, I got it all!

So, how can it happen for you? Believe it or not, there are no official, churchy words to recite in order to have Jesus as the Savior and Lord of your life. It's between you and Him. When you acknowledge Jesus as the Christ, the only Son of God, God then lives in you.

Talk to Jesus. Don't hold back anything. Tell Him simply and honestly what you feel in your heart. Tell Him why you need Him. Jesus forgives. He already knows about you anyway, He just wants to hear it from your lips.

There's no special place, or time, or way to stand or sit or kneel. The most important thing is what is in your heart, because that's where Jesus looks.

You'll find that Jesus is the friend you've always wanted. He always has time for you and always wants to be with you. Jesus never rejects your call for help; He always cares. And even better, Jesus <u>longs</u> for a personal relationship with <u>you</u>.

Maybe you really desire just to know more about this Jesus. If this is you, then we encourage you to email us
  (<u>warren@sonbeams.org</u>) or (<u>marybeth@sonbeams.org</u>) or write us at 408 Colonial Drive, Henderson, TX 75652.
We will get some more information to you.
Note: Anything you say or write to us about stays confidential with us. We do not share your personal information or address with anyone else.

<u>Into His Word</u>

"So you will be saved, if you honestly say, "Jesus is Lord," and if you believe with all your heart that God raised him from death."
                    Romans 10:9 Contemporary English Version

Alphabetical List of Titles

A Brush and Paint 56
A Squirrel Is on Our Cable 88
A Tree on the Next Island 82
Are You Being Friendly or Are You Married? 70
Bailey and Delilah 92
Being a HIT and Mary Beth's Sink 15
Between the Biscuit and Me 67
Come Here, Delilah 72
Cream in My Coffee 26
Disconnected 58
Fillin' Up the Water Bowls 62
Getting In and Out of God's Groove 18
He Doesn't Count the Minutes 28
Holding My Hand over My Other Ear 40
How's Your Reception? 94
I Wanna Be a Cloud 84
In a Dog's Body 77
It's Not Always Opportunity 80
Jesus and the Rusk County Library 21
Lord, Please Don't Hold the Chicken 30
Mary Beth and the Office Ants 44
My Very Next Step 53

Not a Night Light, Please	86
Peek-a-Boo	46
Puppies, Fleas, and God	38
She Called Me Mr. Mary Beth	24
Take One Pill, 2 Times a Day	32
That's Not Sin, You Know	34
The Grasp	101
The Squirrels Are Just a-Diggin'	22
The Water Is Always Hot	91
Their Votes Don't Count	60
There I Was in a Zip Lock Bag	50
There Is No Life in the Fence	74
Throwing Away Cold Coffee	96
Trapped!	64
Wait Till the Coffee Is Ready	36
Weighing in with God	42
What's Making You Dance Today?	99
Your Leaves Don't Have to be Dry	48

A Dirty Sink, A Bug, and Squirrels: God Speaks

My Thoughts _____

A Dirty Sink, A Bug, and Squirrels: God Speaks

My Thoughts _____

A Dirty Sink, A Bug, and Squirrels: God Speaks

My Thoughts _____